Bibhu Prasad Mishra

PREPARING
for a
Winning
INTERVIEW

Bibhu Prasad Mishra
(MBA, Preston University, USA)

V&S PUBLISHERS

Published by:

V&S PUBLISHERS

F-2/16, Ansari road, Daryaganj, New Delhi-110002
☎ 23240026, 23240027 • *Fax:* 011-23240028
Email: info@vspublishers.com • *Website:* www.vspublishers.com

Branch : Hyderabad
5-1-707/1, Brij Bhawan (Beside Central Bank of India Lane)
Bank Street, Koti Hyderabad - 500 095
☎ 040-24737290
E-mail: vspublishershyd@gmail.com

Distributors :

▶ **Pustak Mahal®**, Delhi
J-3/16, Daryaganj, New Delhi-110002
☎ 23276539, 23272783, 23272784 • *Fax:* 011-23260518
E-mail: sales@pustakmahal.com • *Website:* www.pustakmahal.com
Bengaluru: ☎ 080-22234025 • *Telefax:* 080-22240209
Patna: ☎ 0612-3294193 • *Telefax:* 0612-2302719

▶ **PM Publications**
• 10-B, Netaji Subhash Marg, Daryaganj, New Delhi-110002
☎ 23268292, 23268293, 23279900 • *Fax:* 011-23280567
E-mail: pmpublications@gmail.com
• 6686, Khari Baoli, Delhi-110006
☎ 23944314, 23911979

▶ **Unicorn Books**
Mumbai :
23-25, Zaoba Wadi (Opp. VIP Showroom), Thakurdwar, Mumbai-400002
☎ 022-22010941 • *Telefax:* 022-22053387

© **Copyright:** V&S PUBLISHERS
ISBN 978-93-813842-1-3
Edition : 2012

Printed at : Unique Colour Cartan, Mayapuri

Contents

Preface

Preface

$\mathcal{I}$t gives me immense pleasure to present this book before you. The knowledge shared in this book primarily aims to prepare job-hunters to face the challenges of changing corporate environment, and learn the tricks and skills to excel at job front as well as in job interview process.

The title of this book **"Preparing for a winning Interview"** itself speaks about the theme of this book. It sends a message to the readers that to win over the race, one needs to understand and learn basic skills and traits to stand out among the crowd. So be prepared in advance, because it is important to survive in a competitive scenario where meeting deadlines will not leave you with sufficient time to focus on other aspects of job. Therefore, before work pressure and confusion throw you out of the race, be prepared and learn to survive.

Author

Publisher's Note

"Your book bag has transformed into a brief case and your casual attire into business attire; it's time to start thinking like a professional."

Making the transition from College/ University Campus to Corporate World is one of the biggest challenges students face in their career as they confront an inevitable transition from the happy assignments and mid-semesters scenario to team work and deadlines. Moving from an academic environment to a corporate scenario has many changes and one needs to understand the organisational dynamics in order to get well in this new environment as corporate houses prefer to recruit employees who can be immediately employed and deployed.

Training college/ university students to make them more employable is one of the key challenges for most of the companies across the world. So it is evident that companies also feel the necessity to groom the fresh students to make them more professionals and fitted to a corporate setup and that is why companies organise various workshops to groom their employees. However, in most of the cases it is seen that these workshops end in incomplete training and disappointment.

Students and youngsters find it difficult to adapt the necessities of corporate environment primarily because of the vast difference in the way professors and managers operate; while professors focus on increasing learning quotient and improving subject matter understanding; managers want implementation of the knowledge and therefore focus on getting the task done, meeting deadlines, etc. So, while one focuses on learning, the other focuses on significant leverage. This added pressure takes a heavy toll on students and makes it even more difficult for them to scale the success ladder at corporate level. Besides handling these pressures, it is becoming more and more important to have the correct know-how to proceed in career.

To bridge the gap that exists between Campus environment and Corporate setting and to help those students who are just entering the Corporate World or in the threshold of Campus and Corporate, **V&S Publishers** launches its imprint – **Campus to Corporate** which focuses on subjects like Perfecting Corporate Skills, Developing a Proactive Outlook, Fine Tuning Personal Grooming, Time management and Stress handling, Confidently handling Interview and Group discussion and so on.

We look forward to your feedbacks.

PART-I

Interview Preparation

1
Researching About the Interview

$\mathcal{I}$nterviewers describe lack of knowledge about the company as one of their main reasons to reject a candidate. So make a habit of doing your homework.

The employers expect you to know about their organisation and industry. It is quite likely that they will ask you questions designed to test how well you have done your homework. For example, you could be asked one or more of these questions to assess your knowledge of the company:

- What do you think it takes to be successful in this career?
- Do you enjoy doing independent research?
- Do you have any plans for further education?
- Why do you want to work in this industry ?
- What do you know about our company?
- Why are you interested in our company?

Collect Information

Well, the first thing to do is to examine the company's website. Other external sources of information may also be tapped. But don't stop here. Spend some time getting acquainted with the key industry that the company or division operates within. You can find all the resources you need by visiting company website or search about the company in the following:

- Google search
- Annual Reports or other printed materials of the company
- People employed with the company whom you know as part of your network or alumni

Also spend time upgrading your interview skills and style. Do some research to determine the type of interview you should expect during your visit.

If possible, ask the company contact person or his assistant for a copy of the interview schedule and make sure you get the names of those who are interviewing you. Try to find out information about these people. The web is a great source for providing this type of information.

Make sure you know the exact post you are interviewing for so that you have an idea about your duties and responsibilities, as well as salary range.   Determine the qualities so that you can develop the abilities to cope up with the position. Figure out as much as possible about the employer's needs. Learn as much as you can about the company.

Step-by-Step Method to Conduct Research on Companies

One of the most essential skills a job-seeker can learn during a job-search is research skills. The quality of your research skills may make or break your job search. So, improve your research skills. You'll find that research skills will not only help you in searching for a new job, but will come in handy in many other situations in the future.

Information is one of the most crucial aspects of job-search; the more you know the easier it is for you to find information; the more are your chances of success. Employers value job-seekers who possess key information about the company because that knowledge demonstrates your interest and enthusiasm for the company and for the job.

Let's move on a short journey through the basic steps in conducting company research:

Step 1: When to Start Research: For most job-seekers, there are three crucial times to conduct research.

looking to identify popular companies in your industry or even in a particular geographic location.

always best to relate yourself to the company and shape your cover letter and resume for each employer individually.

you'll want to display your knowledge of the company or industry.

The sooner you get started, the better result you will get.

Step2: Information You Need To Know: You have to gather two types of information.

The first type of information deals with general company information. The types of information you might gather here comprise of the following information:

The second type of information deals with the following:

advancement opportunities

functions

Of course, you may also research the industry, key competitors, and countries where the company has offices.

Step 3: Where to Start From: If you really have no idea of what companies might be best for you, there are some good places to start. A number of media groups have already done the research for you - and have produced various 'best' lists like best employer of the year, best private companies, best employee-owned companies, companies ranking in Forbes 500 list, etc.

Step 4: How to Find Company Information: The single best resource of company information is the company's Website. You can find the company site by typing the company name in your browser. For example, if you were trying to find information on Reliance, all you need to do is enter www.reliance.com. and company's website will open. However, not all companies have such obvious web addresses, so the next easiest thing to do is go to your favourite search engine, such as Google.com, and type the company's name in the search box. Then simply follow the link to the company's website.

Sometimes the information you will find on a company's website is limited. Although companies normally place adequate information on their sites, the private companies (not traded on any stock exchange) do not provide sensitive information. The next best solution in such a situation is to read external reviews and profiles of companies.

Another vast source of company information comes from articles and stories published in various media outlets. There are factually thousands of media outlets, from national news and business publications to specialised industry-oriented publications.

Primary Tools for Conducting Company Research

1. Log on to Google.com and find the company's Website. Most public companies have a section of their Websites dedicated to investor relations and often have their annual reports online which can be downloaded easily.

2. Web-Based Secondary Sources can also be used for conducting company research. They include:

Naukri.com - a website that displays large database of openings.

Monsters.com - a job search website.

Jobbala.com - provides a place for people to rate your jobs and to do research on reviews of potential employers from others. It is not designed to be a rant and rave place, but a place where you can anonymously express your feelings about your current and past employers.

TimesJobs - it offers a vast array of opportunities to Indian job seekers. There are several ways to find jobs on this site. You can simply fill in the search form and take a look at the results. You may read lists such as Hot Employers and Featured Employers. You could submit your resume for free and stand a chance to have it seen by one of the 25,000 recruiters that visit the site everyday. Verifying the Job Fair calender is another good option. Career Services are available to job seekers who wish to have professionally written resumes seen by hundreds of placement consultants.

CyberMedia Dice - CyberMedia Dice is a specialty job directory for professionals looking for technology related jobs. Employers can be found in listings like recent job postings, top employers, featured companies, city search and jobs from consultants. Alternatively, you can use the site's search tool and just type the areas or companies you are interested in. Registered members can post their resume online and be sure that it will be seen by potential employers that are truly interested in tech-savvy workers. A useful set of Career resources can be found at CyberMedia Dice. It includes interviews with HR Managers and career planning advice.

Latest Jobs India - it is a website that contains several articles for job seekers. These articles deal with a variety of professional areas, like telemarketing, the taxation sector, human resources, data entry, customer service, accounting and management, to name a few. Academic and scientific Jobs are also discussed and include topics such as biotech career, teaching and research jobs. But the site's most useful resource is certainly the list of sample resumes. There are sample resumes for various types of workers, like quality control inspectors, travel agents, wholesale buyers, technical illustrators, surveyors, telecommunication consultants and technical writers, among others.

ClickJobs.com - ClickJobs.com is an Indian job-seeking portal. It currently offers more than 65,000 job opportunities in different fields. You can register for free at the site and post your resume online. As a member you will be able to save different resumes (each of them for a different area of expertise), apply for jobs via SMS and receive offers in your inbox. ClickJobs.com makes several channels available to its visitors about industries such as technology, marketing, engineering, travel and sales. By going through these channels you will stay informed about the latest news and job offers from top companies.

JobsAhead - visit JobsAhead to have access to plenty of job offers. Highlighted categories include IT, call centre, HR, sales, finance, banking, pharmaceutical, retail and legal jobs. There are also eleven city-specific job listings and cities not covered by them are mentioned in a separate page. By becoming a member of the site, you will have your resume open to more than 10,000 employers and will be able to apply for all jobs online, besides receiving job alerts by email.

3. Web-Based Company Research Links like Yahoo! Business and Economy: Companies provide links to various company websites.

2

Preparing for the First Interview

$\mathcal{A}$s a fresher some people find it very difficult to find a job. There are different types of jobs available and if you have the confidence or if you know how to attend the interview, then you can easily get your dream job.

Here are some tips to follow while preparing for your first interview as a fresher:

• Wear clothes conservatively. Remember to dress in professional manner. Avoid using tattoos, facial piercing and unusual hair colour.

• Give a small introduction about yourself and inform the recruiter that you are thrilled regarding the opportunity of the employment and you are ready to take on responsibilities and challenges offered in the job.

• Offer them a firm handshake. A good handshake helps in forming a good impression about you.

• Talk to the potential recruiter with full confidence. Speak softly and clearly and do not murmur. Give a pleasant smile and stay focused on the discussion.

• Sit straight without crossing your hands and legs. Keep your head high and maintain eye contact with the recruiter through the interview.

• Complete the paperwork correctly and try to avoid making mistakes. Carry the entire necessary details with you, for instance your Identity card, driver's license and work permits etc.

• After finishing your interview do not forget to convey a thank you message to each person you talked to throughout the interview. Declare that you enjoyed talking with them and reaffirm your confidence in your skills to carry out the work.

• If you do not get any reply from the recruiter within a week, follow up with the company by making a telephone call.

Conquering Interview Nervousness

While attending interviews, everyone becomes nervous and this is quite natural. Due to this nervousness or tension many of them can not attend the interview successfully. This mainly happens due to the lack of confidence and self-belief. People usually consider interview as a questioning section by a strange person who will evaluate them by their responses. They do not realise that the interviews are as advantageous for them as for the organisation.

In order to conquer these kinds of problems, first of all, you must prepare yourself mentally for attending the interview confidently. This can be done by boosting your confidence level thinking that this profession is for you alone. To eliminate your nervousness you must do some hard work prior to your interview like preparation for the possible questions that can be asked by the interviewer. Moreover you must be equipped with some information of the organisation such as its accomplishments, future plans, products etc. This is the kind of information that will be more helpful for you in order to prove that you are the right person for this organisation. Another important thing is that at the time of interview you must act confidently even though you are tense.

Before the interview you must be totally stress-free, as stress is one of the main reasons which diminish one's presentation skill. If you cannot reduce stress, then do something that gives you more comfortable and pleasure. Smile has an important role in reducing stress. In fact, smiling is a natural remedy to stress as it discharges endorphins. Or else you can take deep breath. This also makes you fresh and more relaxed.

Go through your resume thoroughly two or three times and be ready to answer all kinds of questions related to your resume.

Helpful Tips to Follow during the Interview

you which are needed for the interview.

exhibits your confidence.

tie or touching your dress repeatedly.

articulate yourself.

Top Five Values Employers Look for in Employees

1. Work Ethics: Employers value employees who understand and possess a willingness to work hard. In addition to working hard it is also important to work smart. This means learning the most efficient way to complete tasks and finding ways to save time while completing daily assignments. It is also important to care about your job and complete all projects while maintaining a positive attitude. Doing more than what is expected on the job is a good way to show management that you utilise good time management skills and don't waste valuable company time attending to personal issues not related to the job. Downsizing in today's job market is quite common so it is important to recognise the personal values and attributes in order to improve your chances of job security as a layoff may occur in the company later during your tenure.

2. Responsible: Employers value employees who come to work on time; are there when they are suppose to be; and are responsible for their actions and behaviour. It is important to keep supervisors abreast of changes in your schedule or if you are going to be late for any reason. This also means keeping your supervisor informed on your progress in all the projects you have been assigned. Being dependable and responsible as an employee shows your employer that you value your job.

3. Positive Attitude: Employers seek employees who take the initiative and have the motivation to get the job done in a set time frame. A positive attitude gets the work done and motivates others to do the same without dwelling on the challenges that inevitably come up in any job. It is the enthusiastic employee who creates an environment of goodwill and who provides a positive role model for others. A positive attitude is something that is most valued by supervisors and co-workers and that also makes the job more pleasant.

4. Adaptability: Employers seek employees who are adaptable and maintain flexibility in completing tasks in an ever changing work environment. Being open to change and improvements provides an opportunity to complete work assignments in a more efficient manner while offering additional benefits to the corporation, the customer, and even the employee. While employees sometimes complain that changes in the workplace don't make sense or makes their work harder, mostly these complaints are due to a lack of flexibility.

Adaptability also means adapting to the personality and work habits of co-workers and supervisors. Everyone has individual strengths and weaknesses and adapting personal behaviours to accommodate others is part of what it takes to work effectively as a team. By viewing change as an opportunity to complete work assignments in a more efficient manner, adapting to change can be a positive experience. New strategies, ideas, priorities and work habits can foster a belief among workers that management and staff are both committed to the same cause.

5. Honesty and Integrity: Employers value employees who maintain a sense of honesty and integrity above all. Good relationships are built on trust. Successful businesses work to gain the trust of customers and maintain the attitude that 'the customer is always right'. It is the responsibility of each person to use their own individual sense of moral and ethical behaviour when working with others and serving them within the scope of their job.

Six Useful Tips on Making Good Impression During an Interview

1. Collect some information regarding the company and the job post for which you have applied. Your knowledge about the company and its ideologies will make a good impression on the person interviewing you.

2. Ensure you look the part. If you are interviewing for an administrative post it may be a bad plan to wear jeans and a T-shirt. Conversely, if you are interviewing for a post as a salesman at the shop, you may not need to wear suit and tie. Get ready to play your part accordingly.

3. When the recruiters introduce themselves, you must stand up, look them directly in the eye, introduce yourself and offer them a firm handshake. Throughout the interview look the interviewers directly in the eye but avoid staring at them. While they are speaking, focus and look directly at them. This gives them an impression that you are listening and are really involved in whatever they are speaking to you.

4. Take notes. It gives the interviewer an idea that you are really interested in this job. Moreover it will help you to note queries if there happens to be a next interview.

performing the interview is a human being. It is acceptable to laugh while they crack some jokes.

6. Do not hunch. Sit straight and concentrate on what they are saying. Moreover, remember never to curse. It is also a good idea to never speak roughly about your present or previous employers.

Handy Skills

That's where handy skills come in. These are the skills you have got your hands on during any activity in your life like jobs, classes, projects, parenting, hobbies, sports, almost anything. These skills are handy and applicable to what you want to do in your next job. During the interview, be ready to point out your handy skills to the interviewers.

Career Portfolio

A career portfolio is a job-searching tool that you develop. It gives employers a complete picture of who you are, your experience, your education, your accomplishments, your skill sets and what you could be. It is much more than just a cover letter and resume. You can use your career portfolio in job interviews to display a point or to explain the depth of your skills and experience.

Your major time might be spent on development of your portfolio, but once you have developed it, keeping it up-to-date should be quite easy. While developing your portfolio, you must determine the format and organisation of the portfolio. Most experts agree that the portfolio should be kept in a ring binder or zipper. You should add a table of contents and use some kind of system - such as tabs or dividers - to separate the various parts of the portfolio.

Apart from the usual portfolio, if you have access to a job-search web site, you may consider developing an online web-based portfolio.

Once the improvement is complete, you then have to gather, write, copy, and assemble the material that goes in the portfolio. This process will not only result in a professional portfolio, but should help you to be better prepared in your job search.

Portfolio Design

Here are some fundamental categories. Don't think you need to use the exact ones for your portfolio. As you consider these items remember that you want to site reasons for the employer to hire you. For this you may need to display your education, work experience, evidence of your work, skills and accomplishments.

Career synopsis and Goals: A description of what you stand for such as work ethic, organisational interests, management philosophy, etc and where you see yourself down the line three to five years.

Professional Attitude / Mission Statement: A short description of the guiding principles that drive you and give you purpose.

Customary Resume: A summary of your education, achievements and work experience, using a chronological or functional format.

Scannable Text-Based Resume: A text-only version of your resume should also be included.

Skills, Abilities and Marketable Qualities: A detailed assessment of your skills and experience. This section should include the name of the skill area; the performance or behaviour; knowledge or personal traits that contribute to your success in that skill area; your background and work experiences that demonstrate your application of the skill.

List of Accomplishments: A detailed listing that highlights the major accomplishments in your career to date. These are one of the most vital elements of any good job-search.

Illustration of Your Work: A sampling of your best work including reports, papers, studies, brochures, projects, presentations, etc. Besides print samples, you can also include CD-ROMs, videos and other multimedia formats.

Research, Publications, Reports: A way to showcase multiple skills, including your written communication abilities. Include any published papers and conference proceedings.

Testimonials and Letters of Recommendations: A collection of written appreciation you have received from customers, clients, colleagues, past employers, professors, etc. Some experts even suggest including copies of favourable employer evaluations and reviews.

Awards and Honours: A collection of any certificates of awards, honours and scholarships.

Conference and Workshops: A list of conferences, seminars and workshops you have participated in and/or attended.

Degrees, Licenses and Certifi cations:A description of relevant courses, degrees, licenses, and certifications.

Professional Development Activities: A listing of professional associations and conferences attended and any other professional development activities.

Volunteering / Community Service: A portrayal of any community service activities, volunteer or work you have done especially if it relates to your career.

References List: A reference list comprises of two to five people including their names, titles, addresses, phone and email etc, who are willing to speak about your strengths, abilities and experience. At least one reference should be a former employer.

Fundamentals of a Good Chronological Resume

To convince a potential employer that you deserve an interview, you probably have about 60 seconds in your hand. So your resume should precisely summarise your accomplishments, your education, your work experience and should reflect your strengths.

A standard chronological resume comprises of:

Your Contact Address: It is essential that a potential employer can reach you easily. This section should include your name, address, phone number(s), e-mail address and a permanent home address.

Job Objective: A job objective is optional and should only be included for new college pass outs and those changing careers. Otherwise use your cover letter to show your career interests and job objective.

If you do use an objective, make sure your objective explains the kind of work you want to do and keep it short with no more than two to five lines.

Accomplishments: The career experts suggest adding a section that highlights your key accomplishments and achievements. Think of this section as an essential summary of your resume in order to identify key accomplishments that will grab the attention of an employer.

Summary of Qualifications/ Qualifications Summary/ Qualifications.

Education: For fresh college pass outs, this should be your next entry. There is emerging a growing trend of employers wanting your GPA or GRADE in this section. If you decide to do so, make sure to use the GPA or GRADE that puts you in the best form. This section should also include school(s) attended (including years of passing), degrees and honours and awards received.

For others with full-time work experience, this section should follow your experience section.

Professional Experience: This section can also be labeled "Experience", "Work History" or "Employment". We like using the term Experience, especially for new college pass-outs, because experience is broader than work history, allowing you to include major school projects that display your skills and abilities.

This section should include company name, your job title, dates of employment and major accomplishments. List experiences in turn around chronological order, starting with your most recent experience.

List your accomplishments in bullet format rather than paragraph format. Avoid discussing job duties or responsibilities.

If you don't have a lot of career-related job experience, consider using handy skills to highlight your work experience better.

Finally make sure to make use of action verbs when describing your accomplishments.

References: This section signals the end of your resume. This section should only include a statement saying references are available if asked upon. Do not include the names of your references on your resume.

Use Action Verbs in Your Resume

Action verbs are the spice to your resume. Without them, your future employer would not know what it was that you were so amazing at doing. Action words help to clarify what tasks, accomplishments and assignments you have done in the past. Never resort to just saying "worked at" or "made sure" or "did this". The lists that you will read below are all presented in past tense, since in your resume if you have completed a task, it should be presented in past tense. If you are still in the process of doing something, write it in the present tense.

You want to captivate your audience and this can be done with less words. Show them the experience and knowledge you have already gained through simply picking appropriate words from the various categories given below:

For Management and Business: Most corporate jobs entail many different roles and responsibilities.Positive action words especially establish the kind of work you have done at your previous job. In the case of business jobs, keeping your language professional and varied is the key to a stellar resume.

For Communication and Public Relations: If you are just out of a communications program from post-secondary education, or your job involved a lot of work with other people, action verbs can show that you've done more than just talking. The importance here is that you show just how well you can communicate and elaborate on your past experiences.

For Technical and Research: It is hard to describe tasks that have jargon and other words that relate to the field in which you are applying without using good action verbs. In the technical jobs you may feel that you should describe the tasks that can purely be labeled as "worked on". But don't fall into this trap!

For Education and Training: As they say, "if you can read this, thank a teacher!" Why not thank a teacher by showing your vocabulary! There are many different ways to show that you have "taught". This is a very good indicator to employers that you are able to lead others and be patient with them. This is a great quality to have if you are thinking of either going into teaching or a job that requires lots of teamwork.

For Teamwork and Collaboration: Remember that you are not supposed to say "we" in your resume. But a lot of times, there are projects, assignments and jobs in general where you are constantly working with others. It would not be fair to just say you have done all the work, so use some good adjectives to show that you have worked in a team but still contributed to their positive successes.

Highlight Your Accomplishments

It might have happened that you have been instructed to list your career accomplishments and you can't think of any. Or you are asked in a job interview, "What accomplishments are you most

accomplishments, but you are unable to recollect them instantly.

The inability to come up with accomplishments happens to lots of jobseekers. Accomplishments are the points that really help sell you to an employer - much more so than everyday job duties and you can pull your accomplishments for job-search success at all stages of the process: resume, cover letter, interview, and more. Career counselors stress that "employers are seeking success stories." It has been observed that resumes are now focusing not only on 'regular' job descriptions, but also include actual, calculable accomplishments.

A resume should be accomplishment-oriented, not responsibility-driven. Such a resume does not grab anybody's attention. People aren't interested in your responsibilities. They already know the general responsibilities of a position so they don't want to know what you do from day-to-day. They want to know that you're a mover and a shaker. They want to learn as to how you contribute to the organisation; how you show initiative; and that you can be a key player. That's what they want to see.

Candidates often write about what their positions entailed and not what they actually did. So they tell employers their job was to do ABC. Employers say.... we need to know what accomplishments you made in your role. This makes you different than another candidate.

Employers would like to know the scope of your responsibilities, size of budget, geographic territory, number of team members you led or were a part of, product lines, and reporting relationship relevant to each of your roles in the previous years.

To a large extent, if a job activity cannot be portrayed as an accomplishment, it may not be worthy of mention in your resume, cover letter, application or even in an interview.

So remember, an awareness of the importance of accomplishments does no good if you haven't been keeping track of all your wonderful achievements.

Lesson One: The minute you start a new job, start keeping track

cards, in a computer database, on a little tape recorder or on your palm device.

But what about all the jobs that have gone by in which you

Lesson Two: Use the following prompts to brainstorm all those terrific things you did.

different from other candidates.

be especially noteworthy.

publications you've produced, products you've developed,

Productivity. How did you contribute to profitability, such as

Increased sales by 60 per cent over the previous year.
Produced total meal sales 30 per cent higher than those of the other servers in the restaurant.
Supervised staff of 27.
Served a customer base of 170, the largest on firm's customer-service team.

Here are some more prompts:

Finally, a word of caution! Resist the temptation to blow your accomplishments out of ratio. Accomplishments should be calculable whenever possible and always provable. Don't risk having a prospective employer call a former supervisor and ask, "Did he

3

Interview Patterns

There are various types of interviews. You need to learn how to get prepared for them separately.

Telephonic Interview

Nowadays most of the companies are conducting interviews over telephone. As an initial stage in a selection process the employers are increasingly using phone interviews as a cost saving screening device, mainly to cut down on travel expenses to bring in candidates from far-off locations. Many of the same principles of interviewing apply to phone interviews, but some aspects are quite different.

Attending Telephone Interviews: Unlike an interview where the date, time, and location are planned beforehand, there is no permanent system for a telephone interview. Some interviewers may tell you in advance when they are likely to call but some may simply decide to lift the receiver and make a call to you presuming that you will be available. At the same time, even you can not be sure as to the person calling is from the HR or any other person from consultancy.

So be well prepared to attend a telephonic interview, if you have sent any application for a job. If they inform you the date and time for the telephone interview then it will be easier for you to get prepared.

Be confident and cool during the telephone interview so you can enhance your performance.

The chief concern of the interviewer, throughout a telephone interview is to assess you by means of your communication skills. Some features that are evaluated during a telephone interview are:

- How better do you speak on the telephone, where you are unable to see your recruiter?
- Do you feel uneasiness if you can not view the recruiter's responds?
- Do you feel confident, skilled, fascinated and excited in spite of the absence of non verbal signs from the other end?

irregular uncomfortable silences throughout the telephone

These are main things that you need to remember while attending the telephone interview. Enhancing the manner in which you speak on telephone is not just how you talk. It is important that you speak relevant things. You can certainly make some positive changes in the way you answer through a smart preparation.

Your preparation must involve thinking through certain queries that you could be inquired with reference to your resume, and how you can attend those answers. But this does not imply that you must learn the answers by heart. It is just that you should prepare a list of expected queries and understand how you will answer them. You can write down points for every answer or just note down some words to explain your ideas.

This kind of preparation will ultimately facilitate you in the real telephone interview by:

individual with proper career strategy and are gravely attracted in the job opening at the company .

If you get caught off-guard as you had not thought through a list of predictable queries your answers are likely to be lengthy, missing attention and you would come out as a puzzled person, which is absolutely not what you wish the recruiter to think.

Therefore, remember the entire points we have discussed here and practice well for your interview. Practice makes you perfect. The more you practice the more successful you become so practice, practice and practice.

Course of Action for Successful Phone Interviews:

interview, be sure you have a professional-sounding outgoing greeting on your voicemail or answering machine. If you have others in your family, ensure that anyone who answers the phone can professionally take a message.

interview with you for practice.

of time so you will be prepared at the exact appointment time. Be sure you schedule as much time as the interviewer needs. If the interviewer calls and wants to do the interview on the spot, tell him or her how much time you have available (if you have any constraints). Offer to call right back or reschedule if you're in the middle of something.

at the time of your phone-interview appointment.

position also enables you to project yourself professionally and helps your voice carry.

gum-chewing, coughing, snuffling, sneezing, throat-clearing. Have a glass of water handy in case your throat gets dry or ticklish. If you feel yourself going off on, for example, an unstoppable coughing jag, ask if the interviewer would like to reschedule.

enthusiasm, smile as much as possible in the phone interview. The interviewer can't see your smile but will hear it in your voice.

during a phone interview, avoid the temptation of reading any of them in response to a question. Have your resume in front of you and organise notes about key questions and aspects of the company in index cards so you can easily access them. Outlines of responses to frequently asked interview questions can serve as loose scripts for your responses. Your goal is brief memory prompts and not full-blown responses to be read. Have a pen and paper handy for taking notes.

doesn't respond at the end of your answer, ask a question to deflect the conversation back to him or her.

candidates, so be prepared for the unexpected. You might be asked questions that throw you offguard. Don't let them make you nervous, and don't feel you must come out with immediate response. Take a moment to think and then respond to the best of your ability.

and move to the next step in the process (usually a face-to-face interview).

sessions do.

Traditional Interview

The usual interview or traditional job interview uses mixed

and "Tell me about your strengths and weaknesses." The success or failure of an interview is more often based on the ability of the job-seeker to communicate than on the truthfulness or content of their answers. Employers are looking for the answer to three vital questions:

Behavioural Interview

It is a relatively new mode of job interviewing. Employers such as AT&T and GE have been using behavioural interviewing for more than a decade now. Because increasing number of employers are using behaviour-based methods to screen candidates, understanding how to shine in this interview environment is becoming a crucial job-interview skill.

The principle behind behavioural interviewing is that the most accurate analysis of future performance is past performance in similar situations. Behavioural interviewing, in fact, is said to be 60 per cent predictive of future on-the-job behaviour, while traditional interviewing is only 15 per cent predictive.

Behavioural-based interviewing is hyped as providing a more objective set of facts to make employment decisions easier. Traditional interview questions ask you general questions such as "Tell me about yourself." The process of behavioural interviewing is much more probing and works in a different way.

In a traditional job-interview, you can typically get away by telling the interviewer what he or she wants to hear, and evading a bit on the truth. Even if you are asked situational questions that

negligible accountability. How does the interviewer know, after all, if you would really react in a given situation the way you say you

to give responses that are untrue to your character. When you start to tell a behavioural story, the behavioural interviewer will typically pick it apart to try to get at the specific behaviours. The interviewer will probe further for more depth or detail such as "What were you

that person," or "Lead me through your decision process." If you have told a story that's anything but totally honest, your response will not hold up through the bombardment of probing questions.

Employers use the behavioural interview technique to evaluate a candidate's experiences and behaviours so they can determine the applicant's potential for success. The interviewer identifies job-related experiences, behaviours, knowledge, skills and abilities that the company has decided are desirable in a particular position.

Many companies look for these characteristics in their prospective employees: decisive thinking, being a self-starter, enthusiasm to learn, deadiness to travel, self-confidence, teamwork and professionalism .

The employer then strikes very sharp questions to extract detailed responses aimed at determining if the candidate possesses the desired characteristics. Sometimes questions are not even framed as queries and they rather typically start with: "Tell about a time..." or "Describe a situation...". Many employers use a rating system to evaluate selected criteria during the interview.

As a candidate, you should be prepared to answer the questions meticulously. Of course, you can prepare better for this type of interview if you know which skills that the employer has predetermined to be necessary for the job you seek. Researching the company and talking to people who work there will enable you to settle in on the kinds of behaviours the company wants.

In the interview, your response needs to be precise and detailed. Candidates who tell the interviewer about particular situations that relate to each question will be far more effective and successful than those who respond in general terms. Preferably, you should briefly describe the situation, what exact action you took to have an effect on the situation and the positive result or outcome.

The Three-Step Process S-A-R:
1. Situation (Or Situation + Task, Challenge, Problem)
2. Action
3. Result (Outcome)

It is also helpful to think of your responses as stories. You may become a great storyteller in your interviews, but be careful not to wander.

It is difficult to prepare for a behaviour-based interview because of the huge number and variety of possible behavioural questions you might be asked. The best way to prepare is to support yourself with some example stories that can be tailored to many behavioural questions. Despite the many possible behavioural questions, you can get some idea of what to expect by looking at the websites that feature behavioural questions.

prepare an effective selection of examples.

Use examples from internships, classes and school projects, activities, team participation, community service, hobbies and work experience as examples of your past behaviour. In addition, you may use examples of special accomplishments, whether personal or professional, such as scoring the winning touchdown; being elected president of your community or organisation; winning a prize for your artwork; leading your team for a project; or raising money for charity. Wherever possible, quantify your results. Numbers always impress employers.

you responded to negative situations. You should have examples of negative experiences ready, but try to choose negative experiences that you made the best of or, better yet, those that had positive ending.

Prepare for Behaviour-Based Interviews:

where you demonstrated top behaviours and skills that employers typically seek. Think in terms of examples that will exploit your top selling points.

accomplishments or meeting goals.

either ended positively or you made the best of the outcome.

your life.

Seeing your achievements in print will revive your memory.

an example out of your folder of tricks that provides a proper description of how you demonstrated the desired behaviour. With practice, you can learn to tailor a relatively small set of examples to respond to a number of different behavioural questions.

and accomplishments so you will be ready with better examples the next time you go on a behaviour interview.

Situational Interview

In situational interviewing, job-seekers are asked to respond to a specific situation they may face on the job. Some aspects of this interview are similar to behavioural interviews. These types of questions are designed to draw out more of your analytical and problem-solving skills at the same time checking how you handle problems with short notice and less preparation.

Situational interviews are quite similar to behavioural interviews, except while behavioural interview focuses on a past experience, situational interviews focus on a made-up situation. For example, in a behavioural interview, the interviewer might start a question with, "Tell me about a time you had to deal with…" In a situational interview, the interviewer asks, "How would you handle this…"

The solution to preparation and success in situational interviews is simply to review your past work experiences and review the steps you took to resolve problems and make corrections. You should also have short stories of some of these past experiences so you can also include them into your answers to show that you have experience handling similar situations.

Here is one way an interviewer might ask an interviewee for a sales manager position: "How would you handle a disobeying team who were not satisfied with the higher management policies, Or, for a management position, a job-seeker might be asked: "How do you handle a dissatisfied employee in your department who has made a habit of arriving late to work and causing minor disruptions during

Stress Interview

The stress interviewing technique is generally used only for positions in which the job-seeker is anticipated to face stress on the job, and the interviewer wants to see how well he or she can handle the pressure. The key to surviving stress interviews is to remain calm, keep a sense of humour and avoid getting angry or defensive.

The interviewer may try to stress you in a number of ways, such as asking six or eight questions in a row; acting rude or sarcastic; differing with you; or simply keeping you waiting for a long period.

Don't take any of these actions personally. Simply stick to your schedule and display your skills and accomplishments calmly. Better, try taking back control of the interview by ignoring the stress. Some experts suggest even getting up and walking around the room so that you may take control by being the only person standing.

Most job-seekers will not encounter such interviews, but it is important to know they exist and learn how to handle yourself if you are faced with such an interview style.

Odd Questions

Another kind of interview stress is illustrated by this example:

suppose you are in a job interview. Everything is going better than you imagined it could. You look professional and fabulous. You are totally prepared. You are on a roll. You're correctly answering every interview question. You feel wonderful rapport with your interviewer. Suddenly, out of the blue he asks you:

"Imagine you could marry anyone for just a week. The person could be famous or not famous, living or from history, real or

It is all you can do to keep your jaw from dropping. You're stunned. You feel your mouth drying up and sweat forming on your forehead. Your head is spinning and your mind is a blank. You are

Welcome to the world of the weird interview questions. The creepy, crazy, gimmicky and off-beat "wild card" questions that seem to have nothing to do with your ability to handle a job. But think, if they are irrelevant to job performance, why do employers

Actually, the employers want to see how well you can think on your feet. They want to see if you will get disturbed or keep your cool. They may want to test your creativity or sense of humour. They want to challenge you. Employers who ask these ridiculous questions no doubt feel the questions do relate to job performance. In creating stress by asking you an odd question, the interviewer may be testing how well you will respond to the stress at the workplace.

And let's face it; job-seekers have vast resources at their disposal in the form of books, articles, and websites on how to respond to traditional and even those tricky behavioural interview questions. The interviewers sometimes want to hit bullet at you by asking a question that you probably didn't prepare for. So get past your pre-programmed answers to find out if you are capable of an original thought.

Of course, I won't refute the possibility that some employers may just be sadistic and want to see you twist or they take pleasure in the amusement of seeing how you'll answer a weird question.

Because the odd questions can be related to anything, hence they are almost impossible to prepare for. Still, some common questions like the one about meeting/dining with a famous person have been around for awhile and could be prepared.

The key to responding to an odd question is not to let it shock you. Don't adopt a (saw-a-snake) look if you get hit with one of these weird questions. Simply smile, take a deep breath and take a moment to compose your response. A little bit of silence is better than coming out with something even sillier than the question. You don't have to outsmart. You don't have to be witty. Just be yourself and give an honest response. If worse comes to worst, and you absolutely cannot think of an answer, ask if you can come back to that question later. You may lose a point on ready answer, but you'll gain points for handling a difficult situation with self-confidence.

If you can turn your answer into something job-related, that's a bonus, but it is probably above the expectations of the interviewer. For example, if you are interviewing for a finance job and are asked what you would do with a large bonus of money, you could give a clever response about how you would invest the cash.

Here are some sample odd questions. The first group is the questions submitted by readers, along with the answers they gave. For your understanding, studying this list of questions may be of no help at all if you're ever asked a weird question because you may be asked something totally different from any of these questions. The point is to anticipate the unexpected and looking over these questions will at least give you the idea of what might be asked and enable you to do a little out-of-the-box thinking about how you might respond when you are asked a bizarre question:

John Peterson, a sales officer at NYL in Canada was asked: "If ghosts appear in front of you and in exchange for anything you desire, offered you any position in their world, what would you

"I thought about this question for a minute," John recalls, "then responded: 'First I would want to go change my clothes since the ghosts just scared the crap out of me! ... then I would ask for a job as marketing manager so I could enjoy marketing the Earth in the ghost world."

Note that these questions have nothing to do with the ability to do a job and are out of line. Some experts suggest not to take these questions as personal rather answer them adding a touch of humor.

Another candidate was asked: "If you could be any animal in

lion so I could be the king of the jungle because it is survival of the fittest in the jungle.." The candidate felt the employer liked his response because he got a second interview.

Some Odd Job Interview Questions:

needs - such as food and water - were taken care of, what two

Case Interview

If you are a Management student, be it BBA or MBA, chances are you already know something about how to handle a very specialised kind of job interview called the case interview. Many Management courses revolve around case analysis, and many business students have become pros at picking business cases apart. Still, the thought of doing so within a tight time-frame (typically 15-20 minutes) in the already highly pressured situation of a job interview can be overwhelming if not downright terrifying.

The case interview is held primarily by management-consulting firms, as well as investment-banking companies, and is increasingly being used by other types of corporations as part of the job-interviewing process. Some firms use case interviews only for MBA-level job candidates while others use them for BBA as well.

Management students who are not totally comfortable with case analysis and fine-arts students with little or no exposure to the case method can take comfort in knowing that a vast collection of resources is available, both on and off the Internet, to tell you everything you need to know to succeed in a case interview.

A case interview is an interview in which you are introduced to a business problem which a particular company is facing. In the interview, you are asked to analyse the situation, identify key business issues and discuss how you would address the problems involved.

Case interviews are designed to examine the skills that are principally important in management consulting and related fields: quantitative skills, analytical skills, problem-solving ability, communication skills, creativity, flexibility the ability to think quickly under pressure, listening skills, business acumen, keen insight, interpersonal skills, the ability to synthesise findings, professional behaviour and powers of influencing people.

Finally, the firm will be looking for someone who can do the real work at hand. Management-consulting companies, for example, want to know that you are the kind of person who can make a good impression on clients. Describing a presentation on case interviewing, experts point out that consulting firms value case interviews because there is no right background for consulting. Consulting requires working in unfamiliar territories, thinking on your feet, and performing in situations where you never have enough time.

Approaching Case Interviews:

books and websites in our resources section for practice

cases. Some companies that use case interviews provide good information on their own websites. Move on to assessing a situation for friends or family members, such as which bank they should choose for a checking account. In all cases, try to avoid "um's" and other such filler words. Practice summarising in a minute or less.

interviewer to ensure your understanding. As some HR experts put it, "Listening is the most important skill a consultant has. The case isn't about you or the consultant; it's about the client."

will allow you to do so. Experts suggest bringing not only a pad of paper but a pad of graph paper in case you want to create a graph as part of your conclusion.

expects you to take a minute or so to collect your thoughts, so don't be afraid of silence. It's a good idea, however, to ask the interviewer if it is alright with him to take a moment to ponder the case. But don't take too much time. Experts agree that five minutes would be excessive.

analysing a case. Your procedure for reaching your conclusions is equally important to the interviewer as is the conclusion itself. In fact, the interviewer wants to watch as much of that procedure as possible so it is vital once you have taken the time to gather your thoughts, to "think out loud" as you are working through the case. Although there is probably not one right answer, some experts warn against "wrong approaches" including "ignoring or forgetting important facts, defending impossible ideas, and forcibly fitting the wrong structure onto a problem."

be interactive. It has to be a two-way-communication with lots of back and forth between you and the interviewer. Questions are expected, especially because the information provided about the case is likely to be incomplete. The interviewer will be looking at your originality in collecting information. Make sure you ask your questions in a reasonable and not haphazard progression. Some experts note that failing to ask questions is a fatal error in the case interview. Also make sure to listen carefully to the answers to your questions. Don't get anxious if the interviewer wants to know why you want the information you are asking for. It's all part of understanding your thought process.

issues of the case. Many of the principles you learned in business school can serve as a framework. For example Five Forces, the SWOT analysis, Value Chain Analysis and the Four P's (Product, Package, Price and Promotion) of marketing. If you have some business experience, you can also draw on applicable situations you've encountered. Make sure your conclusion is grounded in action, not just theory. Be able to explain and defend your reasoning.

to deal with every aspect of the case. As you ask questions, you should be able to pick up clues as to which issues are most important, few of these inkling might be meant to lead you back on track if you have gone astray, so be sure to listen carefully. If direction is not forthcoming, don't be afraid to take control of the conversation. Don't be afraid to think outside the box. Creativity and brainstorming may be just what the interviewer is looking for.

Panel Interview

In a panel interview, more than one person interviews you. The interview panel often sits around a table with you at the head. Make eye contact mostly with the questioner, but scan other interviewers at the same time. And certainly do not ignore any of the members of the board.

After the interview, exhibit confidence and send thank-you notes to all the members of the board.

4

Common Pattern of
Interview Questions

$\mathcal{T}$hese are the common type of questions that are asked during an interview.

Common Questions

Tell me about yourself: Of course, this question is not a question at all but a request for a command performance. It's the most commonly asked interview question, yet it frequently makes interviewee nervous if he is not prepared. The trick is to make your response a brief summary of information that is particularly targeted to the job you're interviewing for.

What are your weaknesses?: Wait! Don't be so truthful and spin your weakness into strength. For example: "I'm a go-getter type and don't believe anyone can do the job as well as I can, so I sometimes have a hard time delegating." That type of response has, however, worn out its welcome with interviewers. Never say you do not have any weaknesses because that may sound unnatural. After all, everyone has a weakness.

An approach that seems to work well is to talk about an area that was once a weakness but that you have worked to improve. Here's how you could frame the go-getter example above in terms of professional growth: "I tend to be a go-getter who has had trouble delegating tasks to others, but I've come to see that teamwork and capitalising on everyone's strengths is a much more effective way to get the job done than trying to do it all myself."

Why should I hire you?: The unspoken part of this question is: "Why should I hire you above all the other candidates?" This is your chance to stand out, to really make a sales pitch for yourself. Describe what sets you apart from other candidates show up your accomplishments, you need to understand that employer will make investment in hiring and training you, so tell the interviewer that this investment will be justified. For example, you could say: "I sincerely believe that I'm the best person for the job. Like other candidates, I have the ability to do this job. But beyond that ability, I offer an additional quality that

about the industry, your previous achievements, how you can do the job better than other, show your spirit and enthusiasm to word the work, what you understand about the current market trends, etc.

What are your strengths?: It is a common question asked in most of the interviews. Speak of those strengths that are very specific to the job you're interviewing for.

Have you ever had a confl ict with your seniors?:Employers might want to see what picture you hold in your mind of your former employer. Don't fall into the trap by speaking your heart out, even if you have any grievances. And if you were never in any sort of conflict with your previous boss, tell how you would handle it if you ever have.

Tell me about your ideal job?: Your description of your ideal job should sound like the job you're interviewing for.

Would your rather work with information or with people?: Ideally, both, but tailor response to job and describe strengths in each area. Don't make yourself sound weak in either area.

What qualities do you feel a successful manager should have?: The question has a two-fold purpose:

Why are your grades not higher?: Don't whine or make excuses. Response should enhance your value as employee. For example:

have hurt your grades, but made you more all-rounded.

but gave you practical work experience.

improve and have learned from the experience.

YES or NO Questions

Never respond with just "yes" or "no." Always elaborate and be prepared to give specific examples. Use fairly current examples. Examples from high school and before are probably too old. Use a variety of examples. Not all from sports, or being an RA, or fraternity/sorority.

THOUGHT Questions

These questions require thoughtful responses and responses that are not self-serving. Try to give responses that are specific to the job.

Questions that Target Your Decision-Making Skills

Be sure your responses demonstrate sound decision-making processes.

Questions about Work Experience

Discuss the key skills you have gained from your work experiences and how these skills will help the employer. This question also gives a good opportunity to talk about your transferable skills if you have minimal experience.

Questions about technical expertise that you lack can be covered up with such statements: "With my experience and background, I feel certain I'll have no problems getting up to speed."

Illegal Questions

It is illegal to ask about age, marital status, children, childcare arrangements, and the like, but employers still come up with subtle ways to ask, such as by inquiring about when you graduated from high school/college. It is best to address the concern behind the question rather than the question itself by saying something like:

"There is nothing about my personal status that would get in the way of my doing a great job for your company." While it may also be tempting to point out the illegality of the question, doing so is not likely to endear you to the interviewer.

Salary Questions

As a screening device, interviewers often ask early in the interview what salary you are looking for. If you ask for more than the employer is willing to pay (or occasionally, on the flip side, undervalue yourself), the interviewer can eliminate you before spending a lot of time with you. That's why the best tactic for salary questions is to delay responding to them as long as possible ideally until after the employer makes an offer.

Try to deflect salary questions with a response like this: "I applied for this position because I am very interested in the job and your company, and I know I can make an immediate impact once on the job, but I'd like to table salary discussions until we are both sure I'm right for the job."

Questions about being Terminated from a Previous Job

It is always uncomfortable to be asked your reasons for leaving a job from which you were terminated. Don't lie about it, but don't dwell on it either. You could explain that you and the company were not a good fit, hence your performance suffered. Or that you and your supervisor had differing viewpoints. Emphasise what you learned from the experience that will prevent you from repeating it and ensure that you will perform well in the future. Read more about handling termination.

Questions about Reasons for Leaving a Current Job

This question is similar to the previous question, even if you haven't been fired. Responses about your relations with the company and differing views from your supervisor can also work here, but remember never to trash a current employer. Always speak positively about past and present employers even if your experience has not been positive with them. Another good response in this situation is to say that you determined you had grown as much as you could in that job and you are ready for new challenges.

Questions about the Future

Interviewees are often asked, "Where do you see yourself down

to this kind of question, with just the right mix of honesty, ambition, and your desire to be working at this company long-term.

Avoid responses such as starting your own business which suggest that you don't plan to stay with the company.

It is not totally inappropriate to mention the personal details like marriage and family but focus mainly on professional goals. Mention your career and company goals first, and tack on any mention of marriage and family at the end.

Your response could be: "I'm here to let you know that I am the best person for the job. If in the future you feel I would be a candidate for a higher level position, I know I wouldn't be passed up."

OR: "I hope to stay at the company and expect that in five years, I'll make a significant advance in the organisation."

OR: "I would like to become the very best employee your company has."

OR: "I hope to stay at the company and expect that in five years, I shall move up the hierarchy ladder of the organisation."

Frequently Asked Questions

In order to give you some idea about frequently asked interview questions, here are some regular questions with some possible answers:

will ask you to give some information about yourself. This comprises your name, address, qualification, work experience, designation in previous organisation and job profile. You must provide the accurate information about your previous designation and organisation.

what you wish to contribute to the organisation. So you must be well equipped with an answer regarding your expectations for the career and what you will contribute for the organisation if you are appointed. You must always be confident while answering the question and never give the impression you have mug up the answer.

Don't talk about the numbers. If they need a choice, just say that you are open to negotiate and await them to mention a number first.

current or past organisation. You must always be optimistic and specific while it comes to telling your previous employer and work responsibilities. You may also need to explain your past work experience and make clear how it links to the post that you are trying for.

skills and how well you face confronts and troubles. Sometimes you will be required to answer certain situational issues simply to check how you solve problems and how efficient you are at finding solutions to issues.

The interviewer will ask lots of questions regarding yourself and your expectations. So ensure that you are well prepared. More prominently, prove that you are knowledgeable and confident. Try to speak positive things and exhibit positive outlooks. A positive outlook will surely help you get the job.

Sixty Common Interview Questions and Answers

Review these typical interview questions and think about how you would answer them. Read the questions listed carefully and you will find some new strategies and suggestions:

1. **So tell me something about yourself?** The most often asked question in interviews. You need to have a short statement prepared in your mind. Be careful that it does not sound rehearsed. Limit it to work-related items unless instructed otherwise.

Talk about things you have done and jobs you have held that relate to the position you are interviewing for. Start with the item farthest back and work up to the present.

For example: My background to date has been centered around preparing myself to become the very best financial consultant I can become. Let me tell you specifically how I've prepared myself. I am an undergraduate student in finance and accounting at (give the name of the university if well known) Delhi University. My past experiences has been in retail and higher education. Both aspects have prepared me well for this career.

2. Why did you leave your last job? Stay positive regardless of the circumstances. Never refer to a major problem with management and never speak ill of supervisors, co-workers or the organisation. If you

leaving for a positive reason such as an opportunity, a chance to do something special or other forward-looking reasons.

3. What experience do you have in this field? Speak about specifics that relate to the position you are applying for. If you do not have specific experience, get as close as you can.

4. Do you consider yourself successful? You should always answer yes and briefly explain why. A good explanation is that you have set goals, and you have met some and are on track to achieve the others.

5. What do co-workers say about you? Be prepared with a quote or two from co-workers. Either a specific statement or a paraphrase will work. For example : "Jill Clark, a co-worker at Smith Company, always said I was the hardest workers she had ever known. It is as powerful as Jill having said it at the interview herself."

6. What do you know about this organisation? This question is one reason to do some research on the organisation before the interview. Find out where they have been and where they are going. What are

7. What have you done to improve your knowledge in the last year? Try to include improvement activities that relate to the job. A wide variety of activities can be mentioned as positive self-improvement. Have some good ones handy to mention.

8. Are you applying for other jobs? Be honest but do not spend a

do for this organisation. Anything else is a distraction.

9. Why do you want to work for this organisation? This may take some thought and certainly, should be based on the research you have done on the organisation. Sincerity is extremely important here and will easily be sensed. Relate it to your long-term career goals.

10. Do you know anyone who works for us? Be aware of the policy on relatives working for the organisation. This can   affect your answer even though they asked about friends not relatives. Be careful to mention a friend only if they are well thought of.

11. What is your expected salary? A loaded question. A nasty little game that you will probably lose if you answer first. So, do not answer it. Instead, say something like, That's a tough question.

interviewer, taken off guard, will tell you. If not, say that it can depend on the details of the job. Then give a wide range.

12. Are you a team player? You are, of course, a team player. Be sure to have examples ready. Specifics that show you often perform for the good of the team rather than for yourself are good evidence of your team attitude. Do not brag, just say it in a matter-of-fact tone. This is a key point.

13. How long would you expect to work for us if hired? Specifics here are not good. Something like this should work: I'd like it to be a long time. Or As long as we both feel I'm doing a good job.

14. Have you ever had to fire anyone? How did you feel about

you like to fire people. At the same time, you will do it when it is the right thing to do. When it comes to the organisation versus the individual who has created a harmful situation, you will protect the organisation. Remember firing is not the same as layoff or reduction in force.

15. What is your philosophy towards work? The interviewer is not looking for a long or flowery dissertation here. Do you have

that works best here. Short and positive, showing a benefit to the organisation.

16. If you had enough money to retire right now, would you? Answer yes if you would. But since you need to work, this is the type of work you prefer. Do not say yes if you do not mean it.

17. Have you ever been asked to leave a position? If you have not, say no. If you have, be honest, brief and avoid saying negative things about the people or organisation involved.

18. Explain how you would be an asset to this organisation ? You should be anxious for this question. It gives you a chance to highlight your best points as they relate to the position being discussed. Give a little advance thought to this relationship.

19. Why should we hire you? Point out how your assets meet what the organisation needs. Do not mention any other candidates to make a comparison.

20. Tell me about a valuable suggestion you have made? Have a good one ready. Be sure and use a suggestion that was accepted and was then considered successful. One related to the type of work applied for is a real plus.

21. What irritates you about co-workers? This is a trap question. Think real hard but fail to come up with anything that irritates you. A short statement that you seem to get along with folks is great.

22. What is your greatest strength? Numerous answers are good, just stay positive. A few good examples: Your ability to prioritize, Your problem-solving skills, Your ability to work under pressure, Your ability to focus on projects, Your professional expertise, Your leadership skills, Your positive attitude

23. Tell me about your dream job ? Stay away from a specific job. You cannot win. If you say the job you are contending for is it, you strain credibility. If you say another job is it, you plant the suspicion that you will be dissatisfied with this position if hired. The best is to stay genetic and say something like: A job where I love the work, like the people, can contribute andcan't wait to get to work.

24. Why do you think you would do well at this job? Give several reasons and include skills, experience and interest.

25. What are you looking for in a job? This could be similar to the answer to your dream job with the exception that here you have to consider the company's profile while conveying your expectations in a job.

26. What kind of person would you refuse to work with? Do not be trivial. It would take disloyalty to the organisation, violence or lawbreaking to get you to object. Minor objections will label you as a whiner.

27. What is more important to you: the money or the work? Money is always important, but the work is the most important. There is no better answer.

28. What according to your previous supervisor your strongest point is? There are numerous good possibilities: loyalty, energy, positive attitude, leadership, team player, expertise,initiativ e, patience, hard work, creativity, problem solver.

29. Tell me about a problem you had with a supervisor? Biggest trap of all. This is a test to see if you will speak ill of your boss. If you fall for it and tell about a problem with a former boss, you may well below the interview right there. Stay positive and develop a poor memory about any trouble with a supervisor.

30. What has ever disappointed you in a job? Don't get trivial or negative. Safe areas are few but can include: Not enough of a challenge; You were laid off in a reduction; company did not win a contract which would have given you more responsibility.

31. Tell me about your ability to work under pressure. You may say that you thrive under certain types of pressure. Give an example that relates to the type of position applied for.

32. Do your skills match this job or another job more closely? Probably this one. Do not give fuel to the suspicion that you may want another job more than this one.

33. What motivates you to do your best on the job? This is a personal trait that only you can say, but good examples are: challenge, achievement, recognition

34. Are you willing to work overtime? Nights? Weekends? This is up to you. Be totally honest.

35. How would you know you were successful on this job? Several ways are good measures: You set high standards for yourself and meet them. Your outcomes are a success. Your boss tell you that you are successful

36. Would you be willing to relocate if required? You should be clear on this with your family prior to the interview if you think there is a chance it may come up. Do not say yes just to get the job if the real answer is no. This can create a lot of problems later on in your career. Be honest at this point and save yourself future grief.

37. Are you willing to put the interests of the organisation ahead of your own? This is a straight loyalty and dedication question. Do not worry about the deep ethical and philosophical implications. Just say yes.

38. Describe your management style. Try to avoid labels. Some of the more common labels, like progressive, salesman or consensus, can have several meanings or descriptions depending on which management expert you listen to. The situational style is safe, because it says you will manage according to the situation, instead of all fitting in one size.

39. What have you learned from mistakes on the job? Here you have to come up with something or you strain credibility. Make it small mistake with a positive lesson learned from it.

40. Do you have any blind spots? Tricky question. If you know about blind spots, they are no longer blind spots. Do not reveal any personal areas of concern here. Let them do their own discovery on your bad points. Do not hand it to them.

41. If you were hiring a person for this job, what would you look for? Be careful to mention traits that are needed and that you have.

42. Do you think you are overqualified for this position? Regardless of your qualifications, state that you are very well qualified for the position.

43. How do you propose to compensate for your lack of experience? First, if you have experience that the interviewer does not know about, bring that up: Then, point out that you are a hard working quick learner.

44. What qualities do you look for in a boss? Be generic and positive. Safe qualities are knowledgeable, a sense of humor, fair, loyal to subordinates and holder of high standards. All bosses think they have these traits.

45. Tell me about a time when you helped resolve a dispute between others? Pick a specific incident. Concentrate on your problem solving technique and not the dispute you settled.

46. What position do you prefer on a team working on a project? Be honest. If you are comfortable in different roles, point that out.

47. Describe your work ethic. Emphasise benefits to the organisation. Things like, determination to get the job done and work hard but enjoy your work are good.

48. What has been your biggest professional disappointment? Be sure that you refer to something that was beyond your control. Show acceptance and no negative feelings.

49. Tell me about the most fun you have had on the job. Talk about having fun by accomplishing something for the organisation.

50. Describe the characteristics of a successful manager. A successful manager should have the vision and capabilities to formulate strategies to reach his or her objectives and communicate these ideas to his or her team members. In addition to serving as a positive role model for co-workers, successful managers must also be capable of inspiring others to recognise, develop, and apply their talents to their utmost potential to reach a common goal. These are the traits I hope to demonstrate when I'm a manager.

51. Do you have a geographic preference? Although I would prefer to stay in this area, I would not rule out other possibilities.

52. Would it be a problem for you to shift base? I'm open to opportunities within the company; if those opportunities involve shifting base, I would certainly consider it.

53. Which is more important to you, the job itself or your salary? A salary commensurate with my experience and skills is important, but it's only one piece of the package. Many other elements go into making up a compensation package, but more importantly, it's critical to me to enjoy what I'm doing, fit into the corporate culture, and feel I'm making a genuine contribution.

54. What steps do you follow to study a problem before making a decision? Following standard models for problem-solving and decision-making can be very helpful. Here are some steps and how they helped solve a problem in a group project:

others.

decision if necessary.

55. How would you describe your leadership skills? You can say: "I am a leader who likes to give the people I am leading the ability to shine. I think it is important to take everyone's opinion into consideration and be willing to listen to what they have to say. I think my job as a leader is to organise things and keep them in order. Being the leader does not mean I know everything there is to know because I can not possibly know more than everyone else about every topic. It is just not plausible."

56. Which is more important: creativity or efficiency? Why? The best answer would be : "I think that the key is a balance between the two, with efficiency being the most important. You could have an extremely creative piece, but if the message of the piece is not clear then it is not efficient and a waste of resources."

57. What two or three things are most important to you in your job? I want to be happy. I want to work in a job that I am passionate about, and for a company that respects and rewards my contributions. I want to have co-workers whom I like and respect. I think these things all work together for a positive work environment which increases productivity ever resulting in happy employees and a happy employer.

58. Have you been fired? Throughout this book we have advised you not to lie. If you have been fired, a lie can look very tempting when faced with this question. However, lying is never a wise course of action, you would be amazed how often people are caught out. The best course of action is to present the truth in the most favourable (but honest) light possible. Have a good explanation worked out and tested with friends.

For instance: 'We had a change in general managers and although I had been doing a great job, as you can see from my achievements, I was replaced by one of his former associates' or 'The company decided to close down its Edinburgh operation and offered me a job in Wales. We would like to stay in the area so that's why I'm looking around'.

59. What is your opinion of the last company you worked for? Stay neutral or positive, no negatives. Try to focus on situations in which you learned and/or contributed something. Running down or insulting your previous employer will make you look far worse than them.

60. Do you have any questions for me? Always have some questions prepared. Questions which represent you as an asset to the organisation are good.

Agreeing that it is impossible to predict exactly what questions a given interviewer will ask of a job-seeker, interviewing gurus nevertheless notes that the secret to success in any interview is preparation. Career experts point out that since few job-seekers prepare for interviews, those who do, will gain a real edge over others through preparation.

You can use these question lists to organise your thoughts about high points you want to share with employers and develop a list of what characteristics might be needed for success in the position for which you are interviewing.

Writing to Learn

Some experts preach that writing is learning because writing enables learners to organise their knowledge and extend it in an organised way so that it remains coherent, unified, reliable.

Composing written responses to interview questions works because it helps candidates learn and remember concepts and content, improve thinking and cognitive abilities, organise their thoughts, enhance communication skills, bolster their self-image and make connections.

The idea of preparing written answers to common interview questions will make job-seekers more confident and allow them to focus their energies on other aspects of the interview while providing detailed, yet concise responses to questions.

Some Writing Tips:

Some of the helpful tips to help out you with your writing skills are:

names properly.

ten or is used to begin a sentence, for example: five years ago, I and my brother.. If the numeral is 10 or greater than 10, it must be denoted in figure, for example: I had 12 matchbox cars.

dialogue or wording and around titles of book.

e-mails to your friends. This is the best way to improve your writing skill.

Feedback will help you to improve your writing skills.

provide your own views on the issues. Visualise arguments you would apply to convince somebody about your views. Conducting speech and seminars will help you think through issues and speak those issues to others.

accurate, specific and simple language.

to improve your writing skills.

may think others are more brilliant, but you know more than you think. Self-confidence and talent will enhance with writing you do.

5
Significance of
Rehearsing and Practising

May be you are a new entrant into the job market who is lacking experience in job interviewing. Or else you are a job-market veteran whose resumes and cover letters yield loads of interviews but you never seem to get the job offer. While these two groups may have the greatest need to polish interview skills, anyone actively interviewing for jobs can benefit from practicing interview skills. A research revealed that a candidate's background and qualifications were far less influential in their hiring decisions than interview performance and professionalism.

Practice will help you reduce interview anxiety, improve your interview skills and in many cases, gain important feedback about how you interview. It will also help you sharpen your communication skills and poor communication skills were the number one turn-off for hiring managers, according to a survey by Society of Human Resource Management. There are several ways to practice before a job interview. They aim at sharpening the interviewing skills.

Mock Interviews

Mock interviews simulate real job interviews and are conducted with a prospective job interviewee and an interviewer, often a career professional who can provide valuable input on your interview performance. The career pro will not only point out your shortcomings, but will acknowledge the areas in which you excelled, thus boosting your confidence. For the inexperienced interviewee, mock interviews provide an excellent picture of what to expect.

You are in competition with everyone else for the job. What will make you stand out? Yes, experience is important and helpful, but it isn't everything. How well you show up in the interview is the other part. The interviewer would rather hire someone with some experience or little experience but who interviewed well as opposed to someone with years of experience but came unprepared for the interview. When you have been interviewed before you know what they are going to ask. So have those answers mentally ready.

The point is, practice all of this at home. Have a friend or spouse ask you interviewing questions so you practice. Be confident. Any good interviewer can sniff weakness and timidity. Remember, interviewing is like anything else. Remember - Practice makes a man perfect. For both of my careers since college, I've got the job

it. How I 'showed up' at the interview was the rest.

While it can be helpful to conduct the interview in a venue where you won't be interrupted, you may actually want your interviewer to create some interruptions to better simulate an actual interview. Take the mock interview seriously, and try to think of it as the real thing. Ask your interviewer to hit you with the trickiest and most difficult questions an employer might ask you.

Consider conducting mock interviews with a variety of people to get some different perspectives. Your friends may be more honest with you about any shortcomings they see in your interview performance.

Videotaped Mock Interviews

Mock interviews provide valuable preparation if you can have them videotaped. A videotaped mock interview that focuses on the non-verbal aspects of your performance - smile, enthusiasm, energy level, personality, confidence, voice, attire, posture, hand gestures, inappropriate body language - can be particularly worthwhile because many people exhibit behaviours while interviewing that they're not even aware of.

At the same time your interviewer can identify your nervous habits which you may not be aware of. You can conduct a mock interview with a friend and have the friend point out only your non-verbals. Or videotape yourself and conduct one review of the tape in which you focus just on the non-verbals.

Some of the bad habits and inappropriate body language you should avoid are:

After a videotaped interview with a career professional, the pro will generally play the tape back so you can both watch and constructively review how you did. Yes, you may cringe at your blunders, but you will learn from them. After all, you may have little time in a real interview to make the right impression. Some HR professionals point out that the interview outcome is determined in the first 60 seconds. "What makes the lasting impression are the silent signals, the facial expressions, the cut of the suit, and the beauty of the speaker."

Observing yourself on tape will help you deal with vocal issues, such as a heavy accent, a baby-soft voice, failure to articulate clearly, speaking too quickly or too slowly, and talking through your nose.

An important key while reviewing the videotaped interview is to put yourself inside the employer's head and note how you come across to the viewer. Are you conveying the demeanor and

your responses, which should be two to three minutes.

Rehearsal

Interview rehearsal is so closely related to mock interviewing that mock interviewing could be considered a subset of rehearsal. But rehearsal also includes the concepts of verbally rehearsing solo for an interview, as well as mentally rehearsing and rehearsing in writing.

One technique is to rehearse these responses aloud by yourself, enabling you to hear how your answers sound and adjust your verbiage as needed. Recording these rehearsals and then listening to the recordings from the employer's perspective can help the prospective interviewee refine and polish substandard responses. You can also try rehearsing in front of a mirror to check out your nonverbal mannerisms.

6

Plan Your Interview Attire

*O*nterview attire is part of your preparation for job interviewing. You can't just go into your closet on the day of the interview and decide what you feel like wearing.

Dress for success

It's probably one of the most overused phrases in job-searching, but also one of the most under-utilised by job-seekers. In job-searching, first impressions are critical. Remember, you are marketing a product - yourself - to a potential employer, and the first thing the employer sees when greeting you is your attire; thus, you must make every effort to have the proper dress for the type of job you are seeking. Will dressing properly get you the job? Of course not, but it will give you a competitive edge and a positive first impression. Here are some questions which you may wish to ask while choosing your attire:

Should you be judged by what you wear? Perhaps not, but the reality is, of course, that you are judged. Throughout the entire job-seeking process employers use shortcuts to save time. With cover letters, it's the opening paragraph and a quick scan of your qualifications. With resumes, it is a quick scan of your accomplishments. With the job interview, it is how you are dressed that sets the tone of the interview.

How should you dress? Dressing conservatively is always the safest route, but you should also try and do a little investigating of your prospective employer so that what you wear to the interview makes you look as though you fit in with the organisation. If you are not dressed appropriately, the potential employer may feel that you don't care enough about the job.

How do you find out what is the proper dress for a given job? You can call the human resources office where you are interviewing and simply ask. Or, you could visit the company's office to retrieve an application or other company information and observe the attire current employees are wearing -though make sure you are not there on a "casual day" and misinterpret the dress code.

Finally, do you need to run out and spend a lot of money on clothes

No, but you should make sure you have at least two professional sets of attire. You'll need more than that, but depending on your current financial condition, two is enough to get started and you can buy more once you have the job or have more financial resources.

Tips

Attention to details is crucial, so here are some tips for both men and women. Make sure you have:

women

Dresses for Women

The standard job interviewing attire for women is a conservative dark navy or gray skirted wool blend suit. Job experts and employers seem split on the notion of pants suits, so a skirted suit is a safer choice.

Other conservative colours - such as beige or brown - are also acceptable. Red is a power colour. A blazer with blouse and skirt is a possible second choice to a suit. You should always wear a jacket.

Skirt length should be a little below the knee and never shorter than above the knee - no nightclub attire here. Avoid wearing a dress (unless accented with a jacket). Blouses should be cotton or silk and should be white, or some other light colour. Shoes should be low-heeled.

Make-up should be minimal, with lipstick and nail polish conservative tones. Pantyhose should be flawless (no runs) and conservative in colour. Avoid both body odour and excessive cologne.

Pantsuits vs Skirted Suits: Whenever I want to watch my students' jaws drop down to their desks, all I have to do is tell them that the "safest" attire for women to wear on a job interview is a skirted suit and that pantsuits - while almost universally acceptable in the workplace - are still somewhat risky attire for interviewing.

My students can't believe it. They are stunned that such a sexist double-standard could still exist in the business world. They are incredulous that they should be expected to wear attire that is so clearly gender-specific.

I can't blame them. I can't disagree with any of their protests. All I can do is prepare them for reality that they might be perceived as less than professional and even lose a job offer if they wear a pantsuit to an interview instead of a skirtsuit. And that they can rarely go wrong by reaching for the highest standard of traditional dress - especially in such conservative fields as banking, investments, and law.

Women should make their own choices about interview attire, but just as with any of the "rules" for dressing for success, they should make those choices fully informed about the risks and realities. Thus, we present the pros and cons of wearing pantsuits to an interview:

Pros

should be acceptable for job interviews.

from a male power structure that seeks to keep women in their place.

looks professional.

you might not interview well. You should be true to yourself, and your clothing should reflect your self-image and help you project your most confident self. Some women feel they look better in pantsuits than in skirted suits.

than skirtsuits because they make women seem powerful and more equal with men.

Cons

wearing a pantsuit, it is almost impossible to go wrong wearing a skirted suit.

is whether the candidate wears a jacket and it is true of both men and women.

interview, but the skirted suit is still the best bet for the first interview. When Andersen Consulting recruits on college campuses, for example, the firm recommends skirted suits for the first two rounds of interviews, with pantsuits acceptable for the third round.

the organisation; if you interview in a pantsuit in a company where all the female employees are wearing skirtsuits, you won't be perceived as fitting in.

indicated that 25 per cent of employers would think twice about hiring a woman who wore a pantsuit to a first interview.

The best strategy may be to ally yourself with the assistant to the recruiter or hiring manager with whom you'll be interviewing. Call up the assistant before the interview and ask about the company culture and whether pantsuits or skirted suits are the norm for interviews. If you really want to wear a pantsuit, but the assistant says it would be out of place, best to stick with the skirted suit. Consider regional differences also. If you're interviewing in an unfamiliar area, be aware that the culture may be different from what you're used to, and it pays to do some research.

skirted suit expectation is outdated and sexist - what can we and men should be asking themselves. This is the 21st century after all.

Say No to...

Dresses for Men

The standard job interviewing attire for men is a conservative dark navy or gray two-piece business suit of natural fibers, such as wool, a white long-sleeved button-down dress shirt, a conservative silk tie that matches the colours in your suit, and nicely polished dress shoes.

If you do not own a suit, or the company is a bit more informal, wear a conservative sports coat (no plaids or wild patterns and preferably a dark colour), nicely pressed dress slacks, a white long-sleeved button-down shirt, a conservative silk tie, and nicely polished shoes.

Your belt should always match your shoes: If you have a beard or mustache, your facial hair should be neatly trimmed. If you have any visible body parts pierced, most experts recommend removing all jewelry, including earrings. Avoid both body odour and excessive cologne.

Say No to...

Finally, check your attire in the rest room just before your interview for a final check of your appearance, to make sure your tie is straight and your hair is combed, etc.

7

Reaching on Time

*A*lways strive to get to an interview early, thus protecting yourself from unexpected delays. Getting to an interview a bit early also allows you time to collect your thoughts and observe people (and corporate culture) while waiting.

Does it really matter if you're just a few minutes late to the interview?

Surveys reveal that if you're even a few minutes late, you're usually eliminated.

What steps can you take to ensure you get to the interview on time?

Make sure you can find the company.

If it's an unfamiliar location, ask for directions, get maps, do a dry run. The Web is a great source for maps.

Allow time to get lost, get tied up in traffic, find a parking place.

How early can I arrive?

Do not arrive more than 15 minutes early. If you get to the location early, kill some time until 15 minutes before.

Making Arrangements

For interviews that require travel outside your immediate area, your first test is one of successfully dealing with the travel arrangements and arriving to the employer's office safely and on time. Every company handles travel arrangements differently, so make sure you clearly understand the procedures and arrangements before you leave for the visit.

Depending on where you live and where the office is, you may have to deal with airlines, buses, trains, taxis, rental cars, maps, tolls, hotels, restaurants, and other expenses. If the company has not prepaid for something, make sure you get a receipt. Consider doing research on the city if you are unfamiliar with the area.

Packing

When packing for the trip, be sure you have all that you need for the time you will spend on the road and at the company - and make sure it's the proper clothing for the climate you are traveling to for the visit.

Finally, do be sure to bring all the necessary job-hunting material, including multiple copies of your resume, a job skills

may need to complete a job application while on the visit.

8

Arriving at the Interview

The interview begins before you even meet the interviewer. It is all about arriving, waiting, and interacting with receptionist

Before the Interview

Realise that those secretaries, receptionists and administrative assistants that you might consider unimportant often play a significant role in the interviewing process. When you enter the reception area or outer office, these gatekeepers who greet you are often asked later by the interviewer to sum up their impressions of you. Learn the gatekeeper's name. We all like to be called by our names, and unless we're frantically busy, we like to be schmoozed. Make friendly conversation with the gatekeepers. You might even ask their advice about the interview. Thank them profusely. Make them feel important – after all, they are.

Even the period when you're sitting waiting for the interviewer can be part of the interview scrutiny. Employers have been known to test candidates by observing what magazines they pick up – a gossip rag or something more cerebral? Others might assess how irritated you get by being kept waiting. Wait patiently without complaint unless the wait is truly unreasonable or you have another pressing engagement. If you have waited an hour, it would be reasonable to ask the receptionist if you can reschedule.

At the Interview

It's something most job-seekers both eagerly anticipate and sometimes dread: the invitation to spend a day or two interviewing at a company's office after an initial interview at a job fair, a screening telephone interview, or after an on-campus recruiting interview(s).

The good news is that you made the cut; the employer thinks highly enough of you and your potential from your initial interview to invite you for the visit. The challenge that lies before you, however, is mastering the informal and formal interviews that await you on the visit.

The purpose of the on-site interview is to allow both you and the employer to gain a more in-depth knowledge of each other - to see if there is a "fit." The employer, through the multiple interviews that occur during your visit, gains a greater understanding of who you are and how you interact with numerous potential co-workers and supervisors. You get firsthand exposure to company's work environment and corporate culture - and prospective co-workers.

An on-site interview is also a great chance for you to really get a snapshot of the organisation's corporate culture. The corporate culture is the environment or personality of an organisation; it dictates acceptable business practices, the treatment of employees, and much more.

Take the time to get a feel for the corporate culture so you can decide whether it's the type of environment where you would feel comfortable working because if you do not fit in with the culture of an organisation, you are simply not going to last long there (or not want to last long there).

9

First Impressions
Last Long

*M*ake the most of the first few minutes of the interview because the job interview is usually your first face-to-face with the employers, first impressions are especially crucial. Never arrive with any kind of food in your mouth or on your teeth, and try not to smoke right before the interview. Turn off your cell phone on the way to the interview.

You finally meet your interviewer. Greet him or her enthusiastically. Stand up (if not standing already) and extend your hand for a medium-to-firm handshake; you want neither the limp, dead fish, nor the bone-crusher. Put on an ultra-warm smile and say something like: "Good morning, I'm glad to meet you" or "Thank you for giving me the opportunity to be a candidate for this position."

Offer a copy of your resume or at least have one handy if interviewer has trouble locating his or her copy.

The interviewer will probably decide whether you are a good fit with the company in the first five minutes of the interview. Much of his or her impression of fit is determined by the rapport or chemistry between you and the interviewer – whether you click with the interviewer. Unfortunately, if you don't, there's a good chance you won't get the job. Even more unfortunately, ways of improving chemistry are limited. You can try making the most of the period of small talk to establish rapport by attempting to find common interests. Look around interviewer's office for clues. If there are family pictures, sports memorabilia or collectibles, comment on them.

In the interview, smiling and making strong eye contact are important elements to establishing a good impression. Answering interview questions with ease showcase your interview preparation and asking questions of the interviewer are vital to making a good impression.

10

Confidence and Enthusiasm

Confidence and enthusiasm can be exhibited through your strong body language. In surveys, interviewers consistently say candidates lack confidence, and especially, enthusiasm. While these traits are to some extent inherent in interviewee's responses to questions and their overall demeanor, the appearance of confidence and enthusiasm can be improved through body language and nonverbal behaviours.

Five Important Body - Language Tricks

- Eye contact with the interviewer, for example, is extremely important! One expert, recognising that eye contact is hard to maintain in a one-on-one situation, says to look at interviewer's nose. Avoid averting your eyes; we've noticed that interviewees often look up at walls and ceiling, as though expecting that answers to interview questions will appear there. Also don't cast eyes downward.

- The best way to show enthusiasm in a job interview is with a big, warm, consistent smile.

- The best way to show confidence in an interview is with a strong, forceful voice.

- Posture can help project confidence and enthusiasm. Sit up straight to look confident. And sit on edge of the seat to appear eager and enthusiastic.

- Hand gestures should be subdued, but make sure you have some gestures to show enthusiasm. Where you might use large hand gestures when making a presentation, use smaller, non-distracting ones in an interview. If you can't keep from talking with your hands and using big, distracting gestures, keep hands in lap or hold a pen.

11

Handling
Tricky Situations

$\mathcal{J}$ob interviewing can be an unnerving experience, but if you know how to handle some of the trickiest situations encountered in interviewing, you can be that much more confident.

The Interviewers

There may be different types of interviewers who present tricky situations before you. Let's first learn about them.

The Bad Interviewer: Not every professional who conducts job interviews with candidates knows how to conduct an interview effectively. In fact some are downright lousy at it. A bad interviewer might be unfocused, disinterested, unprepared. He or she might dominate the interview by doing all the talking or might ask inappropriate and illegal questions.

The Unfocused, Unprepared Interviewer: This type of interviewer has probably not read your resume and maybe can't even find a copy. This hapless soul doesn't even know what to ask you. Be sure to offer this disorganised interviewer a copy of your resume while asking, "May I take you through some highlights of my career?"

The Bigmouth Interviewer: Such an interviewer is holding forth, make as many mental notes as you can (or jot them down if you've brought a small notepad). Don't show your exasperation; instead be an attentive listener and hang on the interviewer's every word. Try to get a word in edgewise by leaning forward and opening your mouth slightly. If that doesn't work, even a nonstop talker will likely eventually ask if you have any questions. At that point, you can ask questions or describe your fit with the company and the position based on the mental notes you've been making.

The Rude, Ill-tempered Interviewer: He may be having a bad day or may be testing you by being unpleasant. Don't let the interviewer's lose their interest on your interview. Keep smiling and respond to questions with as much verve as you would with a cheerful interviewer.

Drawing a Total Blank: What if you simply cannot come up with

hangs there as the seconds tick away, ask the interviewer for a minute to think. If you are truly stuck, ask if you can come back to that question. Such a request is a risky strategy that may eliminate you, but it's better than not answering at all.

Weak Response: Acknowledge your flub and start again, saying, "Here's what I really meant."

Sweating Too Much: Discreetly get out a handkerchief or tissue and dab the sweat. Similarly, if your hands tend to sweat, be sure to wipe them dry before shaking the interviewer's hand.

Informal Interview: Whether it's the night before or the evening afterwards, an informal social event designed for casual conversation is almost always part of the company visit agenda. Employers see this as a time to see how well you seem to fit with their current mix of employees and you should use it as a time to see how this group fits with you.

Some employers put a high degree of importance on this issue, so don't ever forget for even a second that this event is a series of interviews. Don't talk about controversial topics, don't get into arguments, and avoid all other bad habits/manners.

Alcoholic Beverages: During an informal interview you may be offered alcohol. Some career experts say it's okay to have a glass or two of wine (nothing stronger) with a meal, but anything that dulls your senses cannot help you stay sharp and believe me, people will be talking about what you said and did at the meal.

Multiple Interviews in a Day: Make sure you get a good night's rest before the big day of interviews. You will often meet with multiple groups of people, from potential coworkers, to managers and executives. Be prepared for different types of interviews and different style of interviewers. You need to stay focused and excel at each interview session repeating your USP at each interview.

You will find yourself answering the same questions to different groups throughout the day, and while it may seem strange and monotonous, be sure to treat each meeting as a separate interview, even if that means repeating answers you gave in previous interviews. Stay fresh!

Salary: The salary issue is certainly likely to come up. So just make sure you are not the one to raise the salary issue. But you need to be prepared with a response when the issue is raised in one or more of the interviews. Try to stay as flexible as possible in any salary discussion.

homework and know the salary range of the position. If so, use this knowledge to give a desired range, if pinned down for a figure.

Testing: You may be requested to take one or more aptitude or personality tests. The aptitude tests are similar to standardised tests you probably took to get into college and are designed to analyse whether you really have the skills you claim to have. The personality tests are designed to see whether your personality is a fit for whatever personality types of the company is looking for.

12

Asking Questions

*T*oward the end of most job interviews, the interviewer will give you the opportunity to ask questions. You must ask a least one question; to do otherwise often signals the interviewer that you don't really have any interest in the job or the company. Make the most of this key opportunity by asking thoughtful questions.

Questions to Ask at a Job Interview

- Can you describe a typical day for someone in this position?
- What is the top priority of the person who accepts this job?
- What are the day-to-day expectations and responsibilities of this job?
- How will my leadership responsibilities and performance be measured? By whom and how often?
- Can you describe the company's management style?
- Can you discuss your take on the company's corporate culture?
- What are the company's values?
- How would you characterise the management philosophy of this organisation or of your department?
- What is the organisation's policy on transfers to other divisions or other offices?
- Are lateral or rotational job moves available?
- Does the organisation support ongoing training and education for employees to stay current in their fields?
- What do you think is the greatest opportunity facing the organisation in the near future?
- What do you think is the greatest threat facing the organisation in the near future?
- Why did you come to work here? What keeps you here?
- How is this department perceived within the organisation?
- Is there a formal process for advancement within the organisation?
- What are the traits and skills of people who are the most successful within the organisation?

Questions Not to Ask at a Job Interview

On the flip side, do not ask questions where the answer is obvious or readily available or when the topic has already been thoroughly discussed in the interview. Asking such questions demonstrates that you failed to listen to earlier information. Here are some such questions:

raises those subjects.

in terms of job security.

13

Closing the Interview

The wise candidates understand the power of marketing in the job-search, and comparing the job interview to a sales call is vital to achieving greater success in obtaining the job offers you seek. But the burden is not all on the job-seeker, because the employer also sees the job interview as sales call and just as much as you are selling yourself as the product to be purchased by the employer, the hiring manager is also selling the employer's value to you.

And anyone who knows even just a little about sales knows that the key to success is in overcoming objections and then closing the sale. This chapter shows you how you can do the same in the job interview and how using this technique will take you one step closer to the job offer.

First, if you are excited about the job and feel you had a strong visit, you should ask for the job offer. As we say in sales, try to close the deal. If you're offered the job, ask about getting a formal, written offer, and ask about when the company needs your decision.

Second, if job offer talk is still too preliminary, then make sure you ask about the next step in the process and the company's timetable for filling the position.

Overcoming Objections

In sales, it's a proven theory that if you can overcome all your prospect's objections, he will have no choice but to agree to your offer. And while you are not doing exactly the same thing for the same reasons, the logic holds that if you can overcome all the objections of the hiring manager, then you'll be more likely to move on to the next step in the process.

Overcoming objections can be done in a number of different ways, but the keys are to acknowledge the interviewer's objection, understand the true cause of the objection, and respond with enough information to defuse the objection. It's best to anticipate these potential objections before the job interview so that you'll be able to practice your responses.

What do you do if no objections are raised? It might not mean that there are none, so it's best to probe to uncover any, because it's much better to get them out in the open and address them than to let them sit, clouding your future. As the interview winds down, if no objections have been raised, you should consider asking a question such as, "Do you see any concerns that stand in the way of my

Some Common Objections from Employers

Here's a collection of some of the more common objections raised in job interviews.

"We think you have too much experience for this position.": This comment is the most loaded of objections because it can mean one of several things -- and it is your job to discover which one it is. The good news is that if you are in the interview, there is something about your qualifications that make you an attractive candidate. Most often, this comment is concealing a concern about your age, attitude, or motivation. Obviously, the interviewer cannot ask your age, but someone with a lot of experience is often older, and the employer may have some concerns about fit, especially if the rest of the department is younger. Older workers also sometimes put out a vibe that because of their vast experience they know it all and are seen as having an attitude problem. Finally, if you have years in the same type of position, some interviewers will question your drive and motivation to move ahead incorrectly assuming that everyone wants to do so.

"We cannot pay you the salary you are seeking.": Related to the over-experience comment is the salary one. Employers are always concerned about salary and hiring employees that best fit their budgets. They may be interested in you, but the nagging question is whether they can afford you. In this case, it's important to defuse the objection without giving away too much information so that you still have leverage if you do get the job offer.

"You don't have enough experience for this position.": On the other side of the spectrum is a job-seeker who shows potential and thus gets the interview, but with whom the employer has some lingering doubts. Perhaps it is not quite enough years of experience, or perhaps the experience is in a different field. The job-seeker's goal is to show exactly how, regardless of the time spent or where it was spent, that you have the skills to get the job done. One great tool for this objection is a career portfolio, in which you not only can tell the story of how you are qualified but show it as well through examples in your portfolio.

"We think you wouldn't fi t into the team.": So many jobs require workers to participate in one or more teams that it seems inconceivable that a job-seeker would not have experience working in teams, but if for some reason you do not have much experience in teamwork, you must demonstrate that you understand the importance of teams in the workplace and how you can be a team player. Demonstrating your knowledge of the organisational culture will also be a plus in this situation.

Combating The Overqualified Label

There's a dirty little secret in job-searching, and if you're a job-seeker with several years of experience - or worse, in middle management - you may have been exposed to it without even being aware. What is

appear to have one of three flaws: too many years of experience, too much education, too highly paid in current or previous job. Yes, it's the label many job-seekers fear: being overqualified. Overqualified is code for "I will not fit the current position". So be forewarned that it is a difficult label to overcome.

Frequently, you will not even be aware of being labeled as overqualified because you'll simply never hear back from the prospective employer. And before we get too much farther along in this article, let me release some guilt and confess my sins. Yes, when I was a hiring manager, I most certainly had a pile for applicants seen as overqualified - and those applicants files were placed directly into the trash. In my mind, these job-seekers could be classified as one of several types:

The out-of work-desperate-for-any-job applicant: This job-seeker failed to explain why someone who worked at this level years ago would be again applying for a position at this lower level and is seen as someone who leave as soon as s/he got a better offer.

The totally incompetent applicant: This job-seeker had worked at the same level for more years than anyone should without giving a reason why he/she never sought a promotion and is seen as a liability.

The too-full-of-myself applicant: This job-seeker, often older than the hiring manager, comes off as having way too many years of experience and sounding as though he/she was responsible for every major accomplishment in the field.

The way-too-expensive-fool applicant: This job-seeker was currently earning a significant amount more than the very top of our salary range and was seen as someone completely out of touch with reality.

The been-there, done-that applicant: This job-seeker passed this level years ago, and for whatever reasons wishes to return to that level but without explanation and could be perceived as washed-up, burnt-out, and in the worst cases, too old.

Develop a two-part strategy. The first part focuses on your job-search correspondence tools, where you will need to develop a short statement explaining exactly why you are seeking the position given your background. The second part focuses on your sales pitch during the job interview, where you can elaborate on why your experience, skills, accomplishments, and enthusiasm make you perfect for the job.

Ten Tips for Overcoming the Overqualified Label

1. Let your network speak for you. Nothing you could say about yourself is stronger than a recommendation from someone who knows you and can recommend you. The ideal scenario is for you to use your network to find someone within the organisation and let that person make the first pitch for you.

2. Focus more on skills and accomplishments than job titles. Use the employer's own words from the job description to show how your skills match perfectly while at the same time downplaying skills not required for this job.

3. Take salary off the table. Make it clear from the beginning that you are completely flexible about salary and that your previous salary is of no relevance to your current job-search.

4. Reveal financial advantages of hiring you. If you suspect salary will be a concern, use specific examples from your past experiences to show how you increased revenue generation and/or cut costs or realised increased savings.

5. Emphasize teamwork and personality. Demonstrate that you are a team player -- that the success of the team is more important than any of the individual team members.

6. Showcase current or cutting-edge knowledge. Discuss recent training or skill-building that shows that you are adaptable and up-to-date and not stuck in the ways of old.

7. Demonstrate loyalty. One method to attempt to overcome the fear that you will leave as soon as a better offers comes along is to point to your longevity with previous employers.

8. Do what it takes to get the interview. Be prepared to deal with the overqualified issue when you call to follow-up your application and influence the hiring manager on at least giving you a "meeting" if not an interview so that you can make your case in person.

9. Everything in moderation. You should illustrate how you are the perfect candidate for the position without overwhelming the hiring manager with your experience or your ego. Avoid intimidating a younger hiring manager.

10. Express interest, admiration, and enthusiasm. Nothing wins over a hiring manager more than a positive attitude and a passion for the job and the employer.

Final Thoughts

If all else fails, if you have followed the guidelines in this article and are still getting the overqualified label, the one last option you have is to ask the direct question of the hiring manager. Be as blunt and direct as possible and ask for the same in the answer by asking something along the lines of: "What can I do to convince you that I

And by all means, stay as positive and upbeat as possible. If you are not having success, evaluate your performance. And if you have been fired or downsized, review your actions and attitudes to be sure you are not emitting any negative or self-doubting vibes. You may have to encounter such questions for which you should choose your answer carefully:

"I'm concerned about the number of jobs you've held in such a short period of time.": If you have had an unusual number of jobs in the last few years, some interviewers will raise the job-hopper question, so you need to be able to explain the logic of your job history. It's important to note that even though employers are not as loyal to their employees as in the past, they still expect employees to be loyal to them.

"We really like you but are just not sure where you fit.": The good news about this objection is that you have won half the battle because the employer likes you and wants to hire you, but is simply unsure of how to best utilize your skills. The key to your response has to be having the confidence in yourself and the knowledge about the employer to explain clearly why you are a fit for the position you are interviewing for.

"Were you fired from your last job?": Unless the employer has inside information about you or you are currently unemployed while job-hunting this should not be a common objection. However, if you have been downsized or fired from your last job, you should at least anticipate this objection. It's pretty common to be defensive about the subject since no one likes being fired even if you were given the pink slip simply because your job was eliminated. So you need to put that behind you when responding to this objection.

Closing the Interview Carefully

Till this stage you have showcased all points about how you are the perfect candidate for the position and overcome any objections from the interviewer, your final step is closing the interview. How aggressive you are in this step is sometimes the difference between an offer and nothing, but it is up to you to decide how strongly you want to close the interview. At a minimum, you should ask about the next step in the process, how many other candidates there are, and an estimate of the timetable for completing the process, what some marketers might call the trial close, where you are feeling out the interviewer. However, if you truly feel the interview was a good one, that you are a great fit for the position, and that you have overcome all the interviewer's objections, you should ask for the job. In the best case, you'll get the offer and in the worst case, you'll be told you need to wait.

In attempting to overcome these objections remember not to dwell on the objection, but instead, once you are sure you understand it, turn it around to overcome it. If you do have a weakness that the interviewer has uncovered, find a way to turn it into strength. For example, if you have been fired from your last job, find a way to showcase how the experience has given you new insight into making sure your boss knows the contributions you are making.

The words that strike fear in all working persons - fired,

refer to only one thing: you're back in the job market looking for new employment opportunities.

While you may find losing your job hard to deal with, most career experts say the best thing you can do is get right back into the job market - even if you've gotten a severance package - rather than sit around being discouraged. And you shouldn't be discouraged. Look at this firing as a chance to start anew with a better opportunity.

How do you deal with being fired or downsized in terms of

getting you in shape to find an even better job than the one you had previously and what follows is the career tune-up checklist.

Career Tune-Up Checklist

1. **Decide on a career path or change:** If you loved your last position and the industry you worked in, then you can move to the next point. But, if you weren't happy, now is the time to think about a career change. What kind of transferable skills did you acquire

   a college admissions office, but now want to get into sales, you have valuable sales and people skills - transferable skills from one position to another. If you're not sure what you want to do, you should do some self-assessment. You can find some great career assessment tests on the Web.

2. **Tune up that resume:** Ideally, you've been keeping your resume current, but if you have not, now is the time to take a hard look at it. Find some great resumes resources here, then:

   the job from which you were terminated on your resume. In most cases, you should include the job unless you only worked there a short period of time (less than three months). Show an end date of your previous job. Focus on your accomplishments and achievements.

a key accomplishments and transferable skills sections for your resume. Positioning these sections at the top of your resume also means you can downplay your actual employment history or at least make it secondary to your accomplishments and skills. A functional resume, rather than a traditional chronological resume, will also serve this purpose.

(text-only) resume. Since job-hunting has expanded greatly to include traditional methods as well as online methods, you really need to have both types.

work with alumni) to review your new resume and offer constructive criticism. We also offer professional resume critiques.

3. **Resolve whether you are staying or relocating**: Now is the time to think about whether enough opportunities exist where you currently live, or whether you need or want to relocate.

4. **Prepare your own network:** Tell your acquaintances that you are in the job market again. You don't need to tell them you were fired if you don't want to, but don't be ashamed of it either, as labor figures indicate that many people have lost (or will lose) their jobs involuntarily. Your network includes your family, friends, former coworkers, former bosses, neighbors, friends of friends - just about anyone. These people may not be able to offer you a new job, but they may know someone who can, so they play a vital role in your job search. And once you find a new job, make sure you keep networking rather than waiting until you don't have a job to do so. Read much more about the art of networking.

5. **Revisit your references:** Depending on the circumstances surrounding your dismissal, you may or may not have a good reference from your former employer. Now is the time regardless to revisit your reference list. You need to contact

these people, which you might already have done through your networking drive, and inform them that you are again on the job market, and ask if they will still be a reference for you. If you know your former employer might give you a bad reference, it is extremely important that you should have some other people who will rave about your accomplishments and abilities.

6. **Be prepared to work:** It's a clichī , but looking for a new job is now your full-time job. Stay focused and accomplish something every day.

7. **Face the tough question:** Be prepared with an answer when an interviewer asks you why you left your last job. Make sure you can articulate why your last job didn't work out and what you have learned from the experience. Never blame a former supervisor or employer and don't make excuses.

8. **Be prepared for rejection:** You may be a little extra sensitive because of being fired, but remember that there is always a degree of rejection in any job search so don't let it get you

Closing Points

Regardless of your style or how you choose to close the interview, here are some key points to keep in mind:

of at least five skills or traits you want remembered after the interview. Choose something "concrete." When you answer with, "I have great communication skills, and I am a hard worker," you will not stand out.
Example: "I have two skills that are distinctly different but that define my personality. I am a very good pianist and an excellent 'computer guy.' I'm known for my love of keyboards."

references, transcripts, background information, and samples.
Example: "Is there any other information that I can provide that would convince you that I am the right person for this

State your interest in the position. Sound interested and tell what added value you can bring to the job.

Example: "From what you have been telling me about this position, and from what I know about your company, I know that I have the right mix of experience and education to bring value to this position. Based on past experiences I can 'ramp up' quickly and be on board with projects within the first few weeks."

to know the next step for follow up. Ask for the decision date, if possible.
Example: "I'm interested in knowing what the next step in the process is and when you will be making a decision so I can follow up."

back, you will need to know whom to contact and whether the employer will accept calls to check the status.
Example: "I'd like to stay in touch and follow up with you in a week or two to see how the process is going and where I stand. How do you prefer that I communicate with you email

Closing the sale is important, but your closing should be tailored to the position; your personality and interviewing style, and the

which closing is appropriate for you and the situation

And for those of you who do not have experience in sales, one piece of warning. While it is helpful to think of the interview as a sales call, do be careful not to overdo it and not oversell yourself to the point where you actually turn the interviewer off about your candidacy. You need to walk the line between being too modest about your accomplishments and fit with the organisation and talking too much about yourself.

Finally, always remember that the interview really is a conversation between two parties who are both trying to showcase their best points. Your goal is to leave the interview knowing you did your best to sell your unique mix of skills and accomplishments while overcoming any objections raised by the interviewer.

14

Thank-You and Follow-Up Communications

$\mathcal{R}$emember that your work is not done just by finishing the interview. You can't simply sit back and wait for the job offer. So consider these key rules and strategies to follow-up your job interviews. Ask at the end of the interview when the employer expects to make the hiring decision. Obtain the correct titles and names of all the people who interviewed you. Ideally, try to get each person's business card.

Be proactive and consider follow-up a strategic part of your job search process. Follow-up can give you just the edge you need to get the job offer over others who interviewed for the position. Use follow-up techniques to continue to show your enthusiasm and desire for the position, but don't make it seem as though you are desperate. Nearly every career book advises jobseekers to send thank-you letters after being interviewed, but how many do? In the aggregate, only about 5 per cent of those looking for jobs perform this simple yet crucial ritual. Thus, it's time to address some of the frequently asked questions about thank-you letters.

Doesn't it come off as wimpy or even desperate to send a thank-you letter? Won't the employer think I'm sucking up?

No. It's a very rare employer who isn't pleased to get a thank-you letter. Most consider it just common courtesy, a way to differentiate you from the pack, proof that you're really interested in the position, and a way to keep your name in front of them.

Will a thank-you note make or break my chances of getting a job?: Well, probably not in most cases, but it could. Why take the chance? One of my former students told me that after he was hired for his first job out of college, his boss told him that he had wavered between my student and another finalist for the position. But then the boss got a thank-you letter from my student, and it made all the difference. Because of that simple gesture, my student got the job.

Should it be a typed business letter or a handwritten social note?: Studies show it doesn't matter. The important thing is doing it. Tailor your letter to the culture of the company and the relationship you established with the person who interviewed you. If you feel the interviewer and the company call for a formal business letter, send that. If your rapport with the interviewer dictate a more personal touch, send a handwritten note.

What about an e-mailed thank you?: Career experts are not in total agreement about the propriety of e-mailing a thank you, but again, the company's culture should guide you. If people in the company use e-mail heavily, your e-mailed thank you will seem right in step. It's also a fast solution if you know the company will be making its hiring decision quickly. Even if e-mail fits in with the company culture, however, it's a good idea to follow up your e-mailed thank you with a hard-copy version.

So, if "just do it" is the by-word, I don't have to put that much effort into it, right?: Wrong. We've heard of candidates on the verge of being hired getting suddenly discounted from consideration because they sent sloppy, poorly written thank-you letters, riddled with typos, misspellings, and grammatical errors. Writing skills are important in many jobs, and employers don't want to have to teach candidates remedial skills. Spell-check, proofread, and have someone else read over your letter before you send it.

If I interview with several people, do I have to send a thank you to each one?: That's the best approach. You can make it essentially the same letter to each, but vary at least a sentence or two to individualise the letters in case your recipients compare notes.

How soon after your interview should you send a thank-you?: The rule of thumb is to send it within 24 hours of the interview.

Should I bother with a thank-you note if I know the hiring decision will probably be made sooner than I can mail a thank-you letter?: The key word here is "mail." If mail is too slow for the hiring decision, find a faster way: e-mail, fax, air-express, or hand-delivery. In fact, if the interview was local, hand-delivery of the thank-you letter can make a super impression.

What if I do receive an offer faster than I can send a thank you?: Send it anyway to thank the employer for the interview and the offer. Your letter can also accept or decline the offer. An acceptance letter can re-state your understanding or the terms of the offer like salary, benefits, vacations days, starting date, paid training, etc. That way any discrepancies can be red-flagged by the employer and straightened out before you start.

Is there anything you can do to make an even better impression with your thank you?: Find a way to personalise it. If you notice that the interviewer collects elephant figurines, for example, write your thank-you note on a note card with an elephant picture on it. Or send a clipping of an article you think the interviewer would be interested in.

About Thank-You Letters

Nearly every career book advises jobseekers to send thank-you

only about 5 percent of those looking for jobs perform this simple yet crucial ritual. Thus, it's time to send thank-you letter to make a better impression.

Find a way to personalise it. If you notice that the interviewer collects elephant figurines, for example, write your thank-you note on a note card with an elephant picture on it. Or send a clipping of an article you think the interviewer would be interested in.

Finally, if you did not get a job offer, follow-up with a phone

during your visit, but we suggest that you check back in a week regardless if nothing else then to continue expressing your interest in the position.

More Aspects of Follow-up

that they may be getting a phone call from the prospective employer.

get a job offer. Do continue to interview and attempt to find other opportunities.

week to ten days (or sooner, if the employer had a shorter

timetable) to ask about the position. And do continue to build rapport and sell your strengths during the phone call.

employer expects.

to. Remember the adage about the squeaky wheel getting the oil. Just don't go overboard and annoy or bother the employer.

there will be other opportunities for you.

the offer you really want.

do try and turn the situation into a positive by bringing the interviewer(s) into your network, possibly even asking them for referrals to other contacts. Read more about the art of networking.

15

Subsequent Interviews

The interview process at many organisations is not limited to a single interview. Multiple interviews are common and can occur for numerous reasons. Career author Chandra Prasad notes that some of these reasons include having the candidate meet key people not met in the initial interview. Sometimes the initial interview is a screening interview with an organisation's human resources department, while the next interview is with the hiring manager who will presumably be the candidate's supervisor if hired. Sometimes the first interview is with the hiring manager, while a subsequent interview is with that manager's boss, who wants final say over hiring decisions. As Prasad points out, various interviewees may scrutinise the candidate for different criteria; one might look at the applicant's technical skills, while another may assess his/her "fit" with the organisation.

Other reasons that Prasad lists for subsequent interviews are:
- Interviewers do not reach consensus about the candidate and need another look.
- Job is offered to top candidate but declined, so interviewers take another look at next people on the list.
- Interviewee seems qualified, but interviewer is concerned with one or more aspects of the candidate.

Employer decides candidate is not suited for position applied for but wants to interview him or her for a different position. It's gratifying to be called for a second or subsequent interview because you are another step closer to the job. Don't blow it now! The key factor in subsequent interviews is to keep your energy level and enthusiasm up. Don't rest on your laurels or tell yourself that just because you have been called back is a reason to be overconfident. Treat each interview like a new beginning when there is just as much on the line as there was for your first interview.

Some additional guidelines are:
- Do take a practice run to the location where you are having the interview or be sure you know exactly where it is and how long it takes to get there.

interview. While some career experts say your chances are 1 in 4 to get the job at this point, others say you have as much as a 50 per cent chance. Even with the field narrowing, it's important to distinguish yourself and ensure that you stand out above your competition.

Compared to the first interview, a second interview is likely to involve more preparation, more people, more questions, more intensity, and more pressure in addition to more likelihood that you will land the job.

interview. Note any questions or situations that caused you difficulty and plan how you will handle those aspects better in the second interview. Derive confidence from knowing that if you hadn't performed well in the first interview, you wouldn't have landed the second. Think about what made you shine in the first interview, and plan to do more of the same. Further, brainstorm new information you can bring into the second interview, new accomplishments, new examples, new evidence of how much you know about the employer.

interview. Presumably you researched the company before the first interview. Now it's time to delve even deeper into that research using our Guide to Researching Companies, Industries, and Countries. Some experts suggest that talking with company insiders is one of the most productive ways to prepare for a second interview. Before your second interview, consider conducting informational interviews with company folks who aren't the ones who'll be interviewing you. Consult our Informational Interviewing Tutorial to learn more. If you are a college student, particularly seek out alumni from your school or sorority/fraternity who work for the employer. Also be sure you're up to date on developments in your field or industry by reviewing trade publications.

interviews in both individual and group/panel formats making for a long day. You may interview with managers, senior executives, department heads, and prospective team members. You may also get a tour of the workplace and be taken out to eat. For college students, this second-interview day may represent the first time the student has been interviewed in the employer's workplace. Plan to bring ample copies of your resume for all the people you may be meeting with.

be and whom you can expect to interview with. If you aren't given this information when the interview is set up, contact the assistant of the main person with whom you'll be meeting to see what you can find out. If you see that a workplace tour is not included on the agenda, ask if someone can show you around as time permits.

respond to a question, maintain eye contact with everyone on the panel and not just the panelist who asked the question.

with representatives of the prospective employer.

16

Handling Salary Negotiations

$\mathcal{S}$alary negotiation is one of the risky tasks, especially at the time of interview. You need to get a competitive salary, but you do not need to be neglected because of your salary necessities. Most of the people join the organisation with the thought of selling themselves by agreeing for a smaller amount. They think they would have made that little further dealing. Conversely, in circumstances where the applicants have been given payment that are higher than their equivalents in the organisation, feelings of bitterness, hostility and rebel can occur.

Therefore salary negotiation has an important role in any organisation. The negotiation must be performed in a way that makes both the worker and the manager believe that they have done a good contract. Organise yourself to handle a salary negotiation and get the best salary that a profession can propose.

The Negotiation

- Recognise what you are worth. Do research on salary ranges in your company. Realise what other people are making that hold this kind of occupation.
- Prove that your abilities are a plus point to the industry. If you have inimitable skills that will promote the industry, they will be ready to give more payment as you are certain to be an asset.
- Understand what salary level you are contented with. Try to negotiate more, other than you must have a plan on what you are equipped to decide on.
- Prove that you are flexible. If they demand a particular salary amount, let your interviewer know that you can negotiate that rate.
- Never agree to a salary offer immediately. You must take enough time to think the offer earlier than giving the interviewer your ultimate decision.
- Be aware of the present salary ranges in the organisation for similar positions. The salary negotiation process should also

consider the present market situations, the profitability of the organisation and the present conditions in the job market.

more proficient and confident applicants will do negotiation on additional benefit for instance paid mobile phone, stock options, remuneration and transfer expenditure and so on.

refuses to give high salary, you can as an alternative request additional vacation days or a better benefits package.

An excellent negotiation that is professed as reasonable by both parties can be foundation of a powerful and equally useful relationship between the worker and the company. This requires honesty and sincerity on the side of both parties throughout the salary negotiation process

Once the negotiating is ended you should make sure you get a printed and signed proof of the result. You must avoid an ultimatum. However, you can be clear on your outlooks. Get enough time and plan for the greatest result.

Skills of Negotiation

Whether you are negotiating salary for your first interview or trying to get more salary and benefits for your current job, mastering the skill of negotiation can bring a drastic change in your career and personal life. Here are some tips to start you on the road to getting what you deserve at work:

your profession, skill and position.

responsibilities you will be taking, as a part of your work, and prove how good are you for handling the entire job entrusted on you.

are flourishing or hurting economically. If thriving, choose high salary, remuneration and bonus. If not, satisfy with what you get in your hand, but think two times about working in such companies.

skills, achievements, work principles and work experience for high payment.

own time to think and give a reasonable answer.

sure they need to appoint you. In that case you have leverage.

by asking what the range is, so you can make out the limitations.

a win-win circumstance.

arrived at an unacceptable negotiating limit. Never burn your viaducts, but graciously refuse the offer.

work hard to go above and beyond your performance objectives. Don't wait to be handed assignments. Instead, seek out opportunities to grow in your career. An exceptional employee is in a prime position to negotiate.

or two to think it over, time permitting.

verification may expose you.

shows that you are negotiating if you do not obtain them, or try to demand for a top wages.

skills, talents, achievements everything which helps you to do your job well. At the same time, reveal your zeal and interest towards the job.

Negotiating Salary for a New Job

The majority people do not recognise that starting a new job is not all the time just about the manager's bottom line. At any interview you have the right to negotiate the money to meet your expectations. If you are looking for a new career, follow the given tips for salary negotiations so you can receive closer to what you are worth:

particulars the conditions of your pay. If you are being presented a reasonable amount, you might not want to negotiate the earnings for your new career.

as pay scale to realise what other experts with your experience and education are currently making, and to decide the proper salary for you. Presented with the proof, your manager will have a harder time saying "no".

and negotiate wages for a new career. Your manager will be far more likely to think about your counter offer if there are no other applicants being considered for the post.

excellent speaker than writer, converse the topic in person or over the phone. If you possess pen and paper, note down your suggestion instead.

denies to negotiate payment. You might be able to acquire better remuneration, a top sign-on perks, telecommuting time or more paid vacation in lieu of a top remuneration.

are offering, express thanks to the manager and walk off. In many cases, he or she will have you on the telephone the next day, unexpectedly ready to negotiate remuneration for the career.

negotiations. Never put forward any demands, coercion or ultimatums, otherwise you will not be granted a job at all.

the threshold upon which you can't go any lower, you might consent to an agreement that doesn't do you integrity.

while you negotiate remuneration. This simply guides to dreadful feelings and bitterness.

17

Asking for References

$\mathcal{A}$t some point in your working career, a future employer will ask for a list of references. A list of references are people, bosses and supervisors you have worked with in the past that will have a conversation with or write a letter to your future employer about YOU. This means they will have to give their honest opinion about you and hopefully show them what a great worker and person you are.

Helpful Tips

In order to make this process go over smoothly, here are some tips which may come handy:

Choose Reference Carefully: The person you put down as a reference should be someone who will say kind things of your work ethic and your experience with them. If there is any incident or rift between you and this person, it is probably better to pick someone else. You want this person to say good things about you. If you would like, you can ask them about the kind of reference they would write. Being honest and open is the best policy.

Keeping Contact: For the most part, if you are a student you may want to approach one of your teachers, or one of your past supervisors. In this case, it is important to identify yourself to this person. Give them a situation in which you have had contact before like if you visited them recently, or had a chat on a different subject. Introduce yourself through a situation you have encountered with them before, even if it was a mere project. It is a good idea to make sure the person knows who you are and how you would know them.

Buffer Time: Never leave asking a person for a letter of reference or to be a reference to the last minute. It is something they are doing for you above and beyond the record, so you want to make sure you give them enough flexibility to do a good job and to not feel rushed about it. A good idea is to give them a deadline to complete the reference letter before you actually have to hand it in. This way there is a buffer of time in case things get delayed.

Be Polite: Since what they are doing is something very beneficial and nice for you, it is a good idea to always stay courteous and polite. Ask them in a formal nature, either in a letter or by face-to-face interaction. Never ask for a reference letter over email unless it cannot be avoidable. You want to be as genuine as possible with this sort of request.

Give Details: You want to be sure that the reference knows about what you wish to pursue or what you hope of doing. You can provide them with your resume, or just send them some of the information about yourself that they might be interested in knowing. This gives them some background to talk about or write about, plus it makes the experience a little bit more individual, rather than a simple "this person was really great recommendation.

Address it Out: It is great if the reference addresses the letter directly to the person who will be reading it. It looks a lot more professional this way. If you write down who it is from, it looks a little less formal and does not give a good impression.

Thank-You Notes: Always send a thank-you note out to your references afterwards. It was a nice thing that they did for you and the least you can do is to thank them.

18

Job-Searching Etiquettes

*W*hile much focus in job-hunting is placed on networking techniques, resume-writing, and interview preparation one small, but very important aspect of successful job-seekers is often overlooked.

What is it that is so often overlooked by job-seekers and career experts alike? It is the simple rules of proper job-seeker behaviour the job-seeker manners.

This article helps fill that void with 10 tips for job-hunting etiquette. Etiquette sometimes gets a bad rap or is overlooked perhaps because the term seems antiquated. But make no mistake, courteous job-seekers stand above those job-seekers without good manners.

So, how can you make a great impression on your next job-search? Easy! Simply incorporate these tips the next time you are seeking a new job.

Ten Tips

1. Be Polite: Whether it's a networking event, job fair, or other career-related event, showcase your inner strengths by patiently waiting your turn to speak with recruiters or hiring managers, properly shake hands (dry, firm, one-handed shake), and address the each person by his or her title (Dr., Ms., Mr.) and last name (unless the event is extremely informal where you can use first names). There are times in job-hunting in which assertiveness is important to demonstrate your interest in the job, but there is no excuse for not being polite.

2. Dress for the Occasion: For job-search events in most professions, the suit is the expected attire and especially for the job interview. You can do your research and determine the level of attire you need.

3. Be Punctual: One of the biggest etiquette mistakes a job-seeker can make is arriving late. Whether you're simply going cross town or driving a great distance, always know the route you're going to take, take a practice run, if possible, and build in extra time for getting lost, street closures, and accidents. Finally, don't overstay your welcome - even if your return flight is hours away; when the interviews are done, say your thank-yous and leave.

4. Learn to Listen: While a great deal of time is spent helping job-seekers prepare great job-search related communication tools like elevator speeches and interview responses, the art of listening is often overlooked. Ignoring what a recruiter or a network contact is saying so that you can simply throw in another plug for yourself is simply rude.

5. Be Knowledgeable: Appearing ignorant or disinterested about a prospective employer is a major lapse in job-search etiquette. By showcasing your knowledge of the employer (and even the interviewer), you demonstrate how serious you are about the opportunity while also gaining serious etiquette points. Preparation is a key skill to learn.

6. Appear Upbeat: Even if you are having a bad day, do not let outside circumstances affect your demeanor in a job-search situation. A positive attitude which includes things like enthusiasm, smiling, good posture, and strong eye contact can go a long way to making a lasting and positive impression. People want to work with happy, friendly people.

7. Communicate Well: While most job-seekers have learned how to communicate in face-to-face situations, there is often quite a bit of room for improvement in phone and email communications and because more of the job-search has moved into these non-personal methods, you should learn rules of phone and email etiquette. Regardless of the venue, good communication is essential to job-search success.

8. Avoid Interruptions

Before heading into a job-search event, turn off cell phones, PDAs, pagers, etc. At a minimum, the device may distract both you and the person you're speaking with, but some people are also annoyed by this breach of etiquette. And certainly, never, ever interrupt someone so you can answer your device unless you know it's an emergency.

9. Eat and Drink Well: No, this tip does not refer to pre-interview meals, but to understanding and using simple table manners which especially come into play when the interview process spills over to include one or more meals. And besides knowing which fork to use and which water glass is yours, remember not to order the messiest nor most expensive item on the menu and avoid alcohol consumption.

10. Always Show Appreciation: Most studies continue to show that a fairly sizable number of job-seekers do not acknowledge and thank the people they meet in networking events, job fairs, or even job interviews. The simple act of writing a short thank-you note to each person you meet in your job-search can literally be the deciding factor in you obtaining an interview or better, receiving the job offer.

Final Thoughts

Well-mannered job-seekers gain the edge in job-hunting because proper job-hunting etiquettes win the hearts and minds of hiring managers, especially compared with job-seekers who are either rude or simply unaware. By following the above 10 tips for job-searching etiquette, you will be on your way to giving yourself that extra edge that may help you land that job of your dreams.

19

Interview Etiquettes

*W*hile you attend an interview, you are trying to establish that you are excellent and extremely hirable. Other than you are also trying to show that you are just simple and typical. You should appear typical. That implies dressing right, "talking" with the attractive body language and following some set of rules of interviewing etiquette. Follow the given simple interview tips for your interview success.

Interview Etiquette before the Interview

- Keep your hair fresh and combed.
- Nails must be neat and trimmed.
- Try to be conventional and make a mistake on the side of prudence.If the organisation does not follow any dress code, try to wear neat and smart looking dresses.
- Reach at least ten minutes before in your interview venue. The remaining time you can utilise to fill up any applications or forms.
- Switch off your mobile phones before entering into the interview hall.
- Don't think that whoever welcomes you is the receptionist.

Interview Etiquette during the Interview

- Give a professional and positive outlook by being confident and offering a strong handshake to each and every recruiter and addressing every recruiter by name when he or she is introduced.
- Strengthen your professionalism and your capability to converse efficiently by talking unmistakably and avoiding slang words.
- Make use of suitable working.You will not get additional tips for every work which has more than ten letters.Apply technical words only when suitable to the query.

Interview Etiquette after the Interview

interviewer and thank each one by name.

possible.

The bottom line is that you are going to spend a lot of time in the work environment and to be happy, successful, and productive, you will want to be in a place where you fit in the culture; where you can voice your opinions, be respected and have opportunities for growth.

20

Standing Out in an Interview

*P*reparing for an interview can be nail-biting. But be certain that you are eligible for the post. The recruiting members want to know more about your talents and your conduct.

- Dress in a professional manner. It does not mean you should buy costly dresses. Ensure your dress is neat and well fitting.
- Avoid wearing more ornaments and overdoing hair as it sounds old fashioned.
- Have knowledge of the job depiction. Emphasise your talents that match the particulars of the work.
- Be punctual. Get ready for unpredicted traffic delays or direction troubles. Check out the map and find out the guidelines to the interview spot.
- Do research on the company you are trying for. Get something that makes you happy regarding the company. This helps you to answer the prominent "why did you opt for this company" question.
- Be affable and more gracious to each person you meet at the interview spot. Give a firm handshake and a pleasing smile. You should come upon as an amiable and skilled person.
- Take additional copies of resume. Note down some points and ask questions in the interview. You can make an impact on the interviewer as somebody who is skilled and truly interested in the organisation and post.
- Don't forget to thank each and every recruiter after the interview. It will be good to offer shake hands once again to the interviewers. Inquire when you can follow up concerning the status of the enrollment for the job post. Also ask for the business card so you can send them a thank note.

An interview is a conversation between two or more people (the interviewer and the interviewee) where questions are asked by the interviewer to obtain information from the interviewee. Interviews can be divided into two rough types, interviews of assessment and interviews for information.

It is common that you all will be nervous at the time of interview though you have probably spent a great deal of time preparing. However, you should let your practice and preparation become a disadvantage.

Once the interview begins, you must focus on interacting effectively with the interviewer. If you have prepared adequately for the interview, your conduct and responses should effortlessly convey to the interviewer the image you want to project.

It is important for you to know that the interviewer's decision about whether or not you will be invited back for an additional interview which will probably be influenced by your attitude and personality as much as by your qualifications. So although preparation is important, your performance during an interview can make things even better. You should always maintain a smile during the time of interview.

Tips To Overcome Nervousness during the Interview

Get Ready: Collect some information about the company through its website or through its brochure. Obviously, if you have a presentation then study your notes and what you are about to say carefully before stepping up on stage. up in meeting. If you have a job interview, think about what they may ask you and figure out some good answers. Doing this carefully and meticulously can remove a lot of nervousness. It may not always be fun. But being well prepared can be helpful not only to remove nervousness but also to face the presentation or get the job.

Question Yourself: What is the worst that could happen?: What

downhill, not really that much. It's easy to get excessively wrapped up in what is about to happen and blow up the event and possible consequences in your mind until it seems like it's a matter of life and death. It seldom is. Asking a few simple questions can put things into a healthier perspective and calm you down.

Stomach Breathing Exercises: Stomach breathing is a wonderful way to defeat negative feelings and visualisations and return to the present moment. Just taking a few dozen abdomen breaths can change nervous and shallow breathing into a calm and strong alternative. It is quite remarkable how quickly this can change how you feel. Here's how you go about it:

other

slowly through your nose. If you are doing it right, your stomach will expand and you'll feel it with your hands.

so you feel your stomach pull slightly inwards towards your spine.

you should not only feel more relaxed and centered. Your body will also be able to continue breathing in this manner without you focusing on it. And that's it. Continue with your normal day.

Yoga Practice: Here is another yoga practice to bring down your nervousness during the interview. Here's how you go about it:

Arrive Early: Arrive 20-30 minutes before your meeting is expected to begin. This will help give you a chance to get a small sense of the company's environment before your interview begins and will also allow you some time to become better adapt with your new surroundings, which hopefully will promote more of a relaxed feeling.

Begin with a Smile: A smile relaxes both you and the audience. It helps to chase away nervousness. Showing a smile in your face hides your nervousness. When you smile, you look more relaxed and confident, and when you are confident, people are more inclined to believe what you say.

Dress Professionally: Appropriate dressing is very important. A well dressed and groomed appearance can do wonders for that first impression.

fashion statement so a tastefully chosen professional outfit, with suitable accessories like a hand-bag or brief case should be fine. Make yourself comfortable in the dressing.

Visualising: Much of our time is spent habitually visualising what may go wrong in a future situation. This may increase your nervousness. It can also give you the results you imagined or feared through

self-fulfilling prediction If you think you will fail, then you are making it a whole lot harder for yourself to succeed.

Imagining in an optimistic way is definitely a more useful and pleasant way to spend some time with your imagination. Now, you may think that visualizing this way is just improbable but seeing in a pessimistic way is just as improbable Either way, you are imagining what may happen in a possible future scenario. Doing it in a negative way may just feel more realistic because that's what people around you are doing or because It's what you have been doing every day for the last few years.

Here are some handy instructions to help you, when have an upcoming meeting:

and also how great will you feel at this meeting.

time.

visualizing that it has already happened, that the meeting is over with the desired result.

relaxed mood before even stepping into the first, second or twentieth meeting.

The above solutions are the easier ones. The suggestions below are the ones you need more time to incorporate. It may take weeks, months or even years. Over time you can gradually make these ideas stronger parts of your life. And they can make you feel less and less nervous in any situation.

do.

people will think of you and thinking that their criticism is always about you.

much of your attention from day to day on your problems, challenges and triumphs. And that's exactly what the next guy/girl is doing too.

In general, people keep much of their attention on their own challenges and problems. And their criticism is often about something negative in their life rather than about something you did. So don't worry too much about it. Now, it's very easy to fall back into a behaviour where you feel needy and wonder what people may think about you and what you do. But by working on this you can, step by step and over time, become less and less worried or bothered by what people might think. This allows you more inner freedom to do and try what you want since you're not feeling trapped in box of other people's opinions.

A Firm Handshake: Give a firm handshake to the interviewer the moment you enter the room. This indicates your confidence level and personality in total. The handshakes will push off your nervousness. When shaking hands, match the pressure of their handshakes. Do not be shamble or unusual with the way you shake hands. Wait a moment and smile at the interviewer after meeting them.

Good Eye Contact: Maintain a good eye contact with the interviewer. It is a form of non-verbal communication and has a large influence on social behaviour. It shows the personal involvement and creates

contact might make you seem insecure. If you are not used to keeping eye-contact it might feel a little hard or scary in the beginning but keep working on it and you'll get used to it.

Don't Touch Your Face: Avoid touching your face. Don't shake your shoulders and hands. It might make you seem nervous and can be disturbing for the listeners or the people in the conversation.

Stay in the Present Moment: This one ties into the one about belly breathing. When you take those deep, powerful breaths and focus on doing that your mind seems to silence. Your projections of what may happen at the meeting or job interview die out. Nervousness comes from these negative projections of what may happen sometime in the future. Or from what happened in the past, perhaps from the last time you had a meeting or an interview. When you instead focus your attention on what is happening now and the nervousness dies out too. Another way to stay in or return to the present moment is to just pay attention to what is happening right now. Just focus on the scene and the sounds right in front of you. Don't think about the reports you have finish before 5 o'clock, the meeting tomorrow or what you want for dinner. Just pay attention to the present moment and nothing else for a few moments. Make it a habit and try to expand the time you can spend in the present moment before your thoughts drift away again.

Don't Swallow the Answer: While giving the answer for the questions don't swallow the last word of your sentence. This brings down the confidence level and indicates that you are not confident about your answer.

Accept: Many people freeze, stammer or panic when they are asked a question that they don't know the answer to. If you don't know the answer, the best course of action to take is to admit it! Tell the host you can try to find out the answer later. Lying or attempting to make up an answer only serves to make you and the host uncomfortable. Accept your ignorance. Don't give wrong answer and get caught. Don't nod your head too much which indicates that you are hiding your tension through your body language.

Validity: Give valid answer for the questions asked by the interviewer and there may be some stressful questions like a series of harsh, rapid fire questions intended to upset you. Such questions are to check your emotions. During that time don't be very emotional and answer with a cool mind.

Avoid Beverages: On the morning of your interview, try to avoid caffeine as much as possible. Most of the people believe that it helps them to relax, but researchers claim that a lot of caffeine can increase tension levels. Also, when you bar caffeine from your diet on the morning of your interview make sure to keep in mind that coffee isn't the only culprit behind increasing nervousness or agitation but chocolate, tea and cola can also play a significant role because they also contain caffeine.

Practice, Practice, Practice: Practice will also help alleviate nervousness. Obviously it is best to work on mock interviews with a media coach who will offer subjective, professional feedback. The more you practice, take action and put yourself in situations that may make you nervous the more confident you become. You have been there before; you know pretty much what will happen. So you feel more and more comfortable and less nervous.

Extra Tips for a Job Interview

release.

show. You need to convince the recruiter with your skills.

his name correctly.

during the interview!

drink and eat before the interview begins.

job.

bad-mouth any former employer.

floor and not on the desk.

be moderate in using hand gestures.

interviewer.

interviewer.

etc. wait outside the building if they accompany you.

steps are, if they didn't already tell you.

memorable.

Self-Assessment

To make it happen as expected in an interview each individual must make a sincere self-assessment and find out one's areas of both

in overcoming weaknesses and unconscious bad habits of posture or speech can be improved by effort. Shortcomings which cannot be overcome can be accepted and acknowledged so that they do not lead to depression and embarrassment when others notice them. Therefore, coming to terms with oneself and knowing how to deal with one's faults, and how to make the best use of one's knowledge and skills, is another vital element in preparing for an interview. So following these practices will definitely eliminate the unnecessary nervousness and I assure you that you can move through your interview with ease and come off with flying colours.

PART-II
Self Management

1

Essential Personal Skills

$\mathscr{H}$ave you ever recognised the personal skills that you require to become successful in your career? If not, try to make out as soon as possible, because whatever you achieve in your life depends upon your personal skills wherein you are the most excellent. It is essential that those personal skills are harmonizing your enduring objective. If you are offering your services to any institute then one of your top personal skills must comprise one key skill needed to assist your work.

Best Personal Skills

Good Mindset: Every one can learn a new skill very easily but you can not train an adult to change his or her mindset or attitude, because it requires certain timeline to obtain. Each employer and even any client wishes to get a good attitude towards his requirements.

Positive Attitude: If you have positive attitude towards anything then you can achieve your goals in your life. People with positive outlook always have a propensity to uncover good things even in the failures.

Discipline: This is one of the necessary qualities that separate a superior with minor one. It improves your hopes in your career and in your life.

Obedience: This quality is the one that detach a high achiever with a lesser one. It makes your integrity in your career as well as in your personal life.

Cooperation: Readiness to help others.

Planning: Do you possess the ability to imagine and plan cautiously before performing? This helps you with reducing the possibility for costly mistakes, as well as maintaining a stable work-flow going.

Goodwill: This is the ability to think that the others are well-intentioned.

Savvy: This is not related to career awareness, but awareness about colleagues and the working atmosphere. It comprises an ability to read other people's purpose from observed activities and employ these details to direct one's thoughts and deed.

Other Essential Skills

Creativity: Creativity provides you an extra benefit over people who are not using this. Your one plan can be worth one billion dollars.

Infl uence: If you possess this skill then definitely you can become a successful leader. This skill is very essential if you work in politics or on higher business positions.

Alertness: If you possess a propensity to carry out your work with alertness then you will become a realistic person in your career very shortly.

Collaboration: If you have good interpersonal skills and you provide and accept collaboration among your co workers as well as friends then you will become an excellent leader.

2

Develop Your Soft Skills

$\mathcal{E}$very organisation, while it recruits its applicants, focuses on both soft skills and the hard skills.

- Hard skills involve the technical things connected to your area of learning.
- Soft skills are very much required to succeed in one's career.

No doubt both soft skills and the hard skills make a person stand out in the mob. Highly skilled person, those who has excelled in his or her education, may not excel if he or she does not know how to cope up with the people and play a key role in the group. Even the company's project comprises various sorts of people at different levels of proficiency. In order to accomplish success, collaboration plays a key role. In this case, soft skills are as significant pointers of work presentation as hard skills.

Soft skills are the mixture of the entire intra-personal and interpersonal skills of an individual. These qualities contain proficiencies in parts like positive outlook, confidence, leadership, communication skills, accountability, decision making, self-awareness, risk taking skill, self-awareness and so on.

Developing Soft Skills

Be an Excellent Communicator: Conquer the fear of talking before the public. You may have good plans or ideas towards solving a problem, but those ideas can be ignored if you can not communicate properly. Make your point accurately and state your requirements with your colleagues and customers. Listen keenly, focus and take part in the discussion.

Problem Solver: Solve the entire problem innovatively. Take right decisions, be positive and emerge with good ideas.

Prove your Readiness: It will demonstrate your willingness, responsibility and curiosity in taking a keen interest in the company.

Excellent Interpersonal Role: Collaboration and project supervision are more significant in career development. If an individual seems difficulty and aloof then, he will be hostile in the group, organisation and customer. It is very essential to be supportive and get leadership when apposite.

Be Ready to Work Efficiently Under Pressure: Be cool and overcome the pressure that accompanies targets in an effectual manner.

Express your Responsibility: Taking responsibility of any work makes you to stand apart from other people. Generally people like to undertake too much responsibility, as it needs both leadership and problem solving skills.

Prove that You are Accountable: Most people dread this more than you recognise. Being responsible for failures, even if, is a barrier in the improvement of your soft skills. Taking responsibility for failures places you as a person of honesty and gives you the freedom to accept the accolades for successes as well.

Advantages of Soft Skills

chances.

Soft Skill Tips for Professionals

It is very much essential for the professionals to improve their soft skills. It consists of communication skill, time management skill, team work, inter personal skill, leadership skill, problem solving skill etc . Some tips are given below to give some guidelines for the professionals regarding how they can improve their soft skills:

Saying No: Most of the people do not know how to say 'No' to the person who asks for help, for additional work, or help for doing anything. Here are some tips you can use while you want to say no.

If you lack sufficient time because of work pressure, inform you are busy but will consider it later on, or put forward an alternate suggestion probably flagging up an additional skilled employee. A different way to state a full work pressure is inform your calendar is full now. Lastly remember it is reasonable just to say "No." Just bear in mind to keep it professional and considerate.

Good Communication: Good communication is very much essential but on many times the foremost thing out of your mouth will not be the exact point you wish to convey. Pay attention to what the individual you are speaking with is telling you and use up some seconds to dwell on your reply. By stopping and considering a reply you decrease the peril of skipping to end or telling something you may not imply.

Time Management: All of us are in a same condition where we are hurrying to finish an assignment or work with a fixed target. You should know how to manage your time you can fix a time then try to finish your work within that time period. This scheduling will help you to achieve your target. Achieving target is always an added advantage to your career.

Negative Feedback: If you receive any negative remarks from your superior regarding your assignment or task, never take it personally. Take it as an opportunity to turn your negatives into positives. Get

Receive the comment and put an action plan in position for the next time you are in the similar circumstances.

Take a Break: Breaks are arranged for a certain purpose. Too much working will cause strain and tiredness. Utilising your breaks will provide you a chance to take rest and there by you can make yourself fresh and energetic. Have your lunch properly as it makes you more energetic and healthy. Feel free to take your breaks as they are given to benefit both you and your superior.

Tips to Improve Your Soft Skills

Most of the people have the same doubt in their mind how they can improve their soft skills. If you are ready to work it is so effortless to attain. If you want to improve your soft skills first you should realise which skills you are good at and which parts you can improve on. Get some suggestions from your friends and families regarding soft skills and personal attributes. Speak with your co-workers and your boss and ask them to provide you some feedbacks regarding the skills which you can improve on. Once you have recognised the soft skills that you need to improve you can take some steps towards improving it.

You can follow the given tips to improve your soft skills:

precise books on communications, leadership, networking etc, other than it also comprises event histories, biographies, and stories about earlier periods.

your growth.

a coworker or your seniors to help you in recognising if necessary.

is most significant to the job you carry out.

at your task.

admiration.

be perceptible and comforting. It must not be hostile or in a shouting manner.

atmosphere in your workplace and personal life as well.

costs in the workplace, while you are in a team.

and others.

to stand apart from the mob.

Try to spend more time with people whom you feel very difficult to handle. Avoid thinking about your feelings but think of how those people will observe you. Try some different approaches with those people to check whether you can make succesful rapport with them.

3

Improve Your Interpersonal Skills

*I*nterpersonal skills are the basic soft skills that should be possessed by a person in his life. These are the skills that refer to the basic etiquette a person develops in his communication and interaction with others. Interpersonal skills are now a days very essential for all people who are working, because they have more chance to meet more people who are very different. Interpersonal skills are mainly required for people who are in the business fields, for those who are working in BPO sectors where there are more chances to communicate and contact people. Interpersonal skills teach how people relate to one another.

Tips to Improve Your Interpersonal Skills

Smile: A smile on your face always makes others comfort and delivers a positive vibration. When you approach others with a gentle smile it is more pleasing and creates a soothing environment.

Listen to Others: Do not cultivate the habit to talk always. Give way for others also to tell their suggestions and opinions. Never be a dictator in your office or any where. When you start to listen to others, you will learn more things in life.

Appreciate Others' Work: Always practice to appreciate others in their work. Simple appreciations are the boost for any one in their work.

Speak Out Clearly: Never hesitate to tell your opinion to others. If you feel that you have to speak out, feel bold and free enough to tell it out. Be clear when you are speaking too. For example when you are speaking with your higher officials, speak out clearly and use plain English.

Never Complain About Your Work: Never complain about your work. Learn how to enjoy your work. Never develop the habit of complaining about your work to other employees in your office.

Tips to Improve Your Interpersonal Communication Skills

Have you ever experienced any hard time while interacting

enhance your interpersonal communication skill:

gestures with your facial expressions. In certain occasion you may be saying yes, even if your face is evidently saying no. ensure your look and your voice concurs.

statement into a patronising statement.

much required, but there are times when skill is required.

too slow will emit various messages and meanings.

hands will make somebody feel undesirable.

the whole thing proper.

Lots of people are frightened by writing. Nevertheless, there are times when writing is treated as a best means to communicate, and the single mode to get your message across.

4

Communication Skills

$\mathcal{N}$o matter how excellent and valuable your suggestion, it is of no value if you can not share it with other people. Therefore, successful communication is very much required. Nevertheless, the skill to communicate successfully will not come easily to all people, and it needs lots of skills that require more practice.

Fluency

Whenever we speak about communication skills, the most important thing that arises in our mind is fluency. `Fluency' is major basic of good communication. If fluency is major factor in oral communication, good hand-writing is very much essential in written communication.

Whenever we speak about communication skills, the most important thing that arises in our mind is fluency. `Fluency' is the basic of good communication. If fluency is major factor in oral communication, good hand-writing is very much essential in written communication.

Whether we communicate orally or in words, our main intention is to express our ideas to other people. Therefore, an excellent communication skill will, certainly, imply how effortlessly we can express the ideas. This, in turn, implies that message must be explicit, comprehensible and accurate.

Voice Modulation

In order to affix impact to your oral communication, evade flat pitch. You can modulate your voice to match up with your sentences. Your oral communication must comprise low and high pitch with suitable delays among words. You must neither shout nor murmur. Other than, you must be capable of being heard. Also, your expressions and body movements must be according to your words.

Knowledge of Language

If you wish to develop your communication skills then you must have deep knowledge of the language you select for communication.

Moreover good grammatical knowledge is required for both verbal and written communication skill. Grammatical mistakes may sometimes be allowed in vocal communication but not all the time.

If you have the good grammatical knowledge then fluency will automatically come. At first, you will not be fluent but slowly you may obtain it. Uncertainty may be one of the reasons that block

Evaluate your earlier conversation for the errors you did. You can record your talk for this reason or can ask a companion to help you in this issue. Eliminate these errors and very soon you will become fluent. Pay attention to audio-video programs and converse with others in the same language.

An excellent communication skill implies an accurate and unmistakable communication that is grammatically correct and conveyed through modulated accent or in precise and readable hand-writing with your expression related your conversation.

communication is typed one or by electronic means conveyed afterward also you must be careful of proper font size and font style which is legible.

Developing Communication Skills, Style and Speech

Communication consists of diplomatic, diction, words, pitch and tone. You must observe how you communicate with other people. Without being diplomatic, you can not be an efficient communicator. Diplomacy implies ability in managing discussions, managing people etc.

Observe and Recognise Your Style: Communication style is more than the way you speak to other people. It comprises your body movements, your pitch and tone and your vocabulary. You can try to get better communication style, once you recognise it.

Develop Your Pitch and Tone: Once you recognised your style, you must try hard to develop it. Pay attention at the pitch and tone that you use while talking to others. Sometimes high pitch will come in your conversation due to nervous. Work hard in lowering your pitch. Modulation of voice is very much required. Tone of your voice express your confidence level, some people can notify by means of your pitch whether you are annoyed or timid. Have a neutral pitch at the same time try not to feel tedious. As per your surroundings you must try modulating your voice, tone and pitch.

Speaking too fast will be a sign of tension and speaking too slowly will sound tedious, so try to keep a normal speed.

Slow down else everybody will think you are nervous and uncertain of yourself if you speak very fast. But, beware not to decelerate to the point where people start to finish your sentences just to assist you conclude.

Apply proper volume which is suitable for the situation. Talk more gently while you are alone. Talk louder if you are talking to huge groups or across larger spaces.

Pronounce words properly because everyone will judge your capability through your vocabulary. If you do not know how to pronounce a word, avoid using it. Wrong pronunciation gives a bad impression about you.

Make use of gestures while you speak with others as it impresses other people. Use proper gesture which is suitable to the situation.

Vocabulary: You must have a good vocabulary. In general you will be judged by means of the words that you use in your communication. Never use tough words to that you do not know the meaning of. Make use of words that are comprehensible and easy to articulate or pronounce. Pronunciation is an essential part of your vocabulary. It improves your communication skills. If you are unable to pronounce a certain word or are uncertain of its pronunciation, avoid using such words.

As you live in this fast growing world it is very much essential for you to possess a good communication skill. By using the above tips, you can make your communication more attractive and effective.

Enhance Your Communication Skills and Succeed

By improving your communication skills surely you can get succeed in your career as well as in your personal life. In this rapidly growing world, it is very much required to develop your communication skills to go ahead and flourish.

you possess the ability to accept and convey information; a

very significant asset taking into account that information nowadays has turned into a valued asset.

eloquent. Lots of other things are essential for successful communication. You must be familiar with them to advance your communication skills. They also depend on having a keen ear apart from having a way with the oral word. Some tips are here that can help you to enhance your communication.

Being an enthusiastic listener enables you to collect the entire information that you can acquire from a particular talk. Being an enthusiastic listener also implies that you concentrate on what is being spoken and ensure that you understand the point.

to get occupied in the discussion. Make out how to ask queries at any time you feel you lose out on a particular point. Make an effort to use your senses throughout an enduring conversation.

to react. Responding involves the use of your mind earlier than you talk whereas reacting generally entails your feeling. Responding all the time keeps you in control as you mindfully oversee what you want to speak. Reacting, conversely, can allow a talk get out of control, which is not the purpose of efficient communication.

regular practice. Take part in as many debates and collective communications as you can. Try to practice the listening skill also. When you move along, you can see a substantial development on them. If there is not a feasible debate to take part in, you can practice with your friends and family. Efficient communication can be used in various parts of your life, be it at job at game. For all time keep in mind that successful communication is a means of creating good relationships.

will finally get success along the way.

Nine Tips to Improve Your Communication Skills

Communications skill is a much required skill that you should achieve if you really wish to advance in your career. It is very essential in keeping your personal rapport with your relatives, families, friends etc

Follow these helpful tips to improve your communication skills:

1. **Listening Skill:** An essential part of good communication is listening skill. Never try to make an end your conversation if you didn't listen and understand what is being spoken. So listen well and respond properly. If you didn't listen properly you can not replay to other person. Listening skill is the foremost thing you must possess to improve your communication.

2. **Skip to Conclusion:** Never skip to sudden end immediately based on what you have listened. Listen to other person's conversation well so you will be able to create the best opinion.

3. **Take Enough Time to React:** Once you have listened and comprehended what is being spoken, take sufficient time to think and then plan what you want to speak.

4. **Never Think That You Are Right:** Sometimes you may make mistakes. But the most important thing is to admit it and listened to where you have done wrong.

5. **Train Yourself to Focus:** Never allow your mind roam or dream while you are speaking or listening to somebody. It will be boorish to the other people.

6. **Accept Compliments:** While we all long for appreciation, most of the people find it very difficult to get appreciation. Occasionally their response sours the moment for the person who gave the praise also. If anyone admires you in an actual way, express thanks to them. You can admit anybody else that deserves a share of the praise but take what is owing to you without commotion or fake humility.

7. **Express Reverence for Their Answer:** Sometimes, you will not have the same opinion with their reaction, but never drive your differing view at them. While you start talking, ask a query that will flicker a talk, not a conflict. Begin your talk as you need it to continue.

8. **Repeating:** Always ask somebody to say again what they have just talked than trying to assume what he or she is talking. If you can not grasp what the other person is talking, it is better to ask them to say it again.

9. **Observe yourself:** Observe yourself while you communicate with others. Watch your own expression and body language. Try to do this standing in front of the mirror and practice it.

Achieving good communication skills is an enduring learning process and will take time to build up. Through certain practices definitely you can develop your communication skill.

5

Boost Up Your
Self-Confidence

$\mathcal{S}$elf-confidence is an essential key for a successful and effective way of life. A person who is having self-confidence will always be a center of attraction. He or she can accomplish their goals very easily. On the contrary, people who have low self-confidence frequently finish up being losers. You have to boost your self-confidence if you real wish to perform well in your life.

Ten Tips for Developing Confidence Level

1. Self-confidence can be found in people who possess a strong self-esteem they may be familiar with their personal value, and take action accordingly. An excellent method to develop your personal value is to scribble down your achievements each day. You may be astonished to know how many positive work you execute each day in your life, but which you do not observe. Once you begin analysing this record, your self-confidence level will definitely increase.

2. Be aware of your goals, split your aims into smaller, more convenient tasks. Encourage yourself whenever you attain smaller goals. It will improve your confidence level, and it will make you to achieve bigger goals.

3. Get an adviser who can help out you to achieve your goal. Meet up your adviser frequently, and ask for his guidance and help as a routine. You may feel that you are learning some valuable things on a daily basis.

4. Mingle with public who are optimistic and helpful, who give respect and value to you give the same respect and value to them. Stay away from people who are pessimistic and dangerous. Such kinds of people lessen your self-confidence. They will insist you to stick on to your negative self. Finally, you get enclosed in their negative and pessimistic world-vision. Not anything can be more harmful than that. Avoid such people as quickly as you can.

5. Focus on how you find happiness in wearing new clothes and being well prepared. It makes you to feel good about yourself.

   every one likes to be found in the group of elegant, smart, clever, successful and optimistic people. You also can become eye-catching if you give out a smart, positive out look. It can be easily differentiated between success and failure.

6. Don't get scared of failures. Get them in your pace and move ahead. Tell yourself that next time you will accomplish something. Don't commit the mistake of enabling your failures to overpower you. They will destroy your self-confidence. An easy method is to shrug your flaws as something insignificant, and undertake a new confront. Certainly, you should learn from your errors, and be practical regarding your talents. People who try to bite off more than you can chew often fail. You must not permit this one to occur in the name of self-confidence.

   exercises regularly. A healthy and strong person is more energetic and attains more in his career and personal life. Physical strength, like self-confidence, shines on your face.

8. Have some interest to know what is happening around the world share this knowledge with your friends. Don't concentrate only on your task and on your troubles. Redirect your concentration to interesting things, and interesting tasks. This will make your mind happy and help you to improve your self-confidence.

9. Participate in some activities in which you are excellent, you might have shined at certain things in the earlier period and then discarded them due to shortage of time. Come back to those activities once more and observe the growth of your self-confidence.

10. Develop new hobbies or skills that keep you engaged. It helps you to improve your self- confidence when you become more expert in it.

Put into practice all these guidelines as truly as you can, and be the witness to the differences that happen in your life.

Self-Confidence in Just Five Days

Day One: Face Yourself: Move ahead and face yourself, irrevocably .Stand before the mirror and look at you for some time. What

nasty to speak, get it off your chest now. Then let it go off.

Day Two: Practice On Your Ego: Standing in front of the mirror looks at you and be ready to turn your words around. Do you remember the old proverbs-"Three put-ups for one put-down". Put that into practice in your restroom. Each negative word you said former times wants to be disproved, removed and wiped out by good qualities you notice in yourself.

You have to state them loudly. I need you to memorise what respects sound like. I wish you to distinguish between the sincere remarks uttered loudly, and the negative talks that restrain you out of fear.

Day Three: Keep The Music Alive: Occasionally, what is within your brain can drown out the entire good in the earth. Teach yourself to act the contrary. Pay attention to your favorite songs, whenever negative thoughts come into your mind play the music, as it keeps you away from the upsetting things. If you are in an angry mood, play an intense song. Depending on your mood select the music and listen to it, it may refresh you.

Compel yourself to imagine in emotions versus words, as frequently the terms we select don't truly speak about how we feel. They evade feeling out of the fear of pain and jump directly to censure.

Censures steal from us self-confidence. Soreness helps us observe who we really are.

Day Four: Laugh Out Loud: Your negative talk begins to panic. It

astonishing how far our subliminal will go to stop development just to evade the perils that rise with change.

Occasionally this ends in an all around fetid mood. A bad temper that keeps you away from associates and crouched at home, that on its own can damage numerous goals, which consecutively directs to self flaw and distrust.

on the television, or going out to watch a comic film. Humors, cartoons, funny stories, they all create laughing. And laughing is indubitably the best remedy for an ailing psyche.

Day Five: Be Amenable To Greetings: If any, the middle point will be the toughest part of the riddle to admit. You have set up ways of handling the negative talks from outside your own head. A successful way to join in encouraging inner discourse however is to fantasy, and makes separate optimistic talks. Once you strengthen their voices, it is easier for them to speak on their own.

If you listen daily, you can see lots of people giving you greetings you didn't observe before. "Thank you" by itself can improve your confidence. Hold these and replay them all through the day in your mind. Mostly good-looking young lady or handsome man may become an all-time friend .When time goes on you can add to the cast of characters. Just like relatives, parents, associates, and tutors can start pessimistic space in your mind, so can they fill up with caring

by anybody else. The selection or choice is yours.

Preparing a Speech

and essential information, but also will help make you as a professional in your field. When you move to the stage, you will be thankful for each bit of attempt you have made.

speech so it includes exact points that will notice and help these particular spectators.

while you research and write down your speech. Expand the topic with less than four or five main sub points.

some important points and think of what you have to speak. Remember all the valuable points that are essential to the speech.

and strength, and striking information.

make many opportunities.

your position again after you take a look at the spectators. Marking some important points with different colours will highlights. In the borders, mark presentation reminders for instance "Speak with poise" and "take breaths!"

plan, for instance printed copy in the occasion of apparatus failure.

short. While the closing stage is near, the speech must progress quickly.

"purchase our product" or "unite us in this cause" or "regard me as a specialist in this field".

over the fixed time. Remember that after twenty to twenty five minutes; even the most active spectators may fall asleep. Concise, clear, excellent speeches all the time beat long, tortuous ones. If your speech is very short, end with a question and answer phase.

Visualise yourself succeeding. Imagine yourself delivering a great speech. Doing this will help you to improve your mind set before giving your speech.

Practising Your Speech

Once you have prepared the speech, next step is practice so practice well in order to ensure that it is a smooth delivery. Why should

you perfect in your presentation. Through practice you can exactly calculate the timing of your speech, ensuring that it fits within the time period you have been fixed. Only in practice you can experience the energy of your speech prior to the real event. Follow the tips given below to practice your speech successfully:

Never sit at your table or computer screen and read your speech. Rather than, stand up. Move around before your imaginary spectators.

will conduct your speech. Ask some friends to come and sit in the chairs and present it before them. If you perform your speech before some friends, instead of by yourself, you can enhance your confidence in presenting it before the spectators or strangers afterward.

real speech, use them in your practice also. This will make you more comfortable with your visual aids when the real time comes to you. Moreover, practicing with your audio-visual aids and props makes you to work out whichever technical problems that may occur.

wear during your real performance. This manner, you can make out if any of your clothes restrain your motion or adds any difficulty to your performance.

voice modulation. Make out which one looks more natural and which one feels uncomfortable. After you have recognised the ones you plan to use in your presentation, rehearse them until they are faultless.

a bit faster than you performed in your rehearsal. You should create allowances for these possibilities in your rehearsal. Normally, it is more satisfactory to descend a bit short of the time period than it is to exceed that limit. However you must not go down the fixed time by more than a minute or two. Fix the time accurately while you practice your speech.

satisfaction. Practice makes you to give an effective speech and moreover you feel confident and enthusiastic.

Delivering a Speech

Most of the people are very much scared to deliver a speech in front of a huge crowd. For them delivering speech is more fearful than death. But some people have innate power they may not feel any hesitation to give a speech. But certain point in our lives every one has to overcome that anxiety and terror to attain the aim of public speaking.

Giving a speech is not difficult task as we think. Many people find it very difficult to face it as they lack confidence and proper practice. Practice is one of the best and easiest ways to prepare yourself for speech. If you are well prepared you can speak just as a normal conversation. So keep on practicing your speech to get a positive result. Moreover excellent body language and voice modulation is the key formula for an effective speech. So try to master in these aspects. Here are some tips to follow.

body language and voice modulation is the key formula for an effective speech. So try to master these aspects. Here are some tips to follow:

position where you can see them without difficulty.

the viewers, pause and start your speech.

expressions and pronunciation, and a clear frame of mind.

you. Don't shout for the sake of being loud.

spectators, including the last line.

your hands in your pockets and use your hands freely.

take your own time to speak.

wherever necessary. This will allow the spectators more time to think about your points.

enough time to understand the points. Moreover, make use of

normal and comfortable gesticulations and facial expressions to give emphasis to particular points.

and pitch to keep the speech energetic and more attractive.

however evade reading from your remarks directly if you are not reading a lengthy quote.

main points of your speech. Give your audience extra time for further thought and leave your spectators with good memories of your speech.

confidently leave the stage.

Giving Better Introduction to Your Speech

openingtoyourspeech. Itisessentialnomatterwhoyouaretalking before to catch the attention of your spectators through using high-impact private relations. Some tips are here to follow.

somebody, speak to your listeners individually.

presentation. Concentrate on power, clearness, facial expression, body movements and correct pronunciations. Try to practice it standing in front of the mirror.

you use the correct intonations promptly. Raise your tone on main parts and decrease your tone to make intrigue and take the spectators in. Moreover, have an honest friend to observe your introduction and get feedback from them.

would not be talking if somebody didn't feel you had something to speak about the subject of importance. Try to be yourself.

narratives. A direct individual experience will assist you relate directly to the listeners.

opening, select three vital topics that tell the listeners "I can make out your requirements."

to give speech. The manner you move to the podium signifies lots to the viewers about whether what you want to talk is worth listening to.

If you possess a general link like being from the same city or having contrary or the same likes or dislikes, for instance a sports team, take them to you by explaining these things.

speaker.

made in your beginning. Whoever introduced you must have completed this previously.

active speaking zeal. Allow the spectators feel the interest you have about the topic.

Handling Question and Answer Session

Every one of us knows that good speakers use lots of methods to attain their goals. However, great speakers have been disrupted by the dreaded Q & A session. So prepare well to handle this section in your presentation. You require lots of practice and preparation to handle this section. Or else you feel some difficulty to handle this section smoothly. So follow the tips given below to handle the Q & A session effectively in your speech presentation:

answers prior to your presentation.

you will be handling questions in the last part. This will help to avoid listener's disruptions that will make your speech tough to follow.

query and that you will arrange additional rounds of queries if time allows. Never allow any one of the audience to dominate the section.

particularly if there is a huge spectator. This not only makes sure that you understood the query, but also offers you enough time to think about your answer should you need it.

who asked the question as the whole audiences are listening to you. Once you finish answering look back at the person, their facial expression will tell you whether they are satisfied with your answer.

with just `yes' or `no' as it seems indifferent. If the query is complicated, respond as briefly as possible and ask the person to meet after the discussion.

that each person has listened to the query properly; moreover it will provide you time to prepare your answer.

the questioner, and then expand your view to the rest of the listeners.

of queries or as you are forthcoming a fixed target. Hang around until you present an excellent answer to a query, and then tell your listeners that, apologetically, you have run out of time.

Research

Try to find the answers to the following questions:

About Audience:

What kind of story will help you get your message across to the

The more you know about the people in front of you, the better you'll know how to connect with them!!!

About Your Surroundings:

Be a Good Speaker

and mentioning the word "you" (meaning the audience). These words refer to emotions. So try to connect with the word and the emotion.

know about a subject, but they are interested in knowing how your information can help them solve their problems! Think in terms of BENEFIT!

Never try to impress them just for the sake of impressing them.

not the whole concept!

words!

problem that the audience has for which my information is the

irrelevant detail, an implicit moral at the end, and a topic that the audience can understand.

some real action in it!

questions as they come up throughout. This allows you to end the presentation with your strongest point. But you need to be extremely comfortable in your talk, so that you can stop and start it without problems. It makes your audience feel as if they are involved in the creation of your speech.

make them stand up and testify, have them undertake small group activities, make them write down ideas/goals on cards and then explaining it to a neighbour.

convey at each turn of the story.

etc only if he/she stimulates you imaginatively and emotionally. It will help you to overcome your own limitations.

practice speaking to that distant person so that he has no difficulty understanding you, using the first few lines of the speech.

if you use them.

beforehand. Go to the front of the room, where you'll begin your talk. Look around. Work all the way around it. Look at the stage, or the place you'll be speaking from, from every possible position an audience member will occupy. Look at the lighting from various angles.

demands something more than words.

charts. If you use words, keep them to a title or some bulleted concepts. Otherwise it's just distracting the audience and raises the risk that the audience will find it more interesting than you.

a scenario to which you return again and again of yourself succeeding brilliantly.

front, left and right, and the back.

of your body to follow your feeling naturally.

can't get close to the audience - still try to get close to it. Move to the very edge of the stage. Grab the microphone; leave the podium and the stage to wade into the audience. It makes you feel closer to your audience.

a couple of times in your mind, until it's clear and precise.

possibly distract your audience or looks more interesting than you. If this is the case, try to remove it.

some ready at your table.

smile confidently, and take charge of the space and the audience immediately.

audience what to do about it.

on. This is meant by listening to the audience.

question! You could do that by adding eg. "Is that a fair way

whether she/he believes that you've answered the question well.

almost any question. Audiences will not think you're stupid if you say "I don't know." But it shouldn't happen all the time.

prizes. Competition makes up an audience and releases huge amounts of energy.

long as they are related to your talk, and personalised as much as possible to the specific audience.

These are weak ways to end. Instead, save a bit of your speech for the close - the best bit. End with a stirring call to action, or your favourite story that makes a compelling point.

audience to be completely sure the speech is over.

hard beforehand that during the speech you can let go of yourself and focus on the receiving end - the audience.

but what the audience hears.

6
Leadership Skills

$\mathcal{L}$eadership is a method through which a person influences other people to achieve objectives and leads an organisation to build it more unified and consistent. An excellent leader receives the talents needed by an efficient manager, exemplifies the qualities of a good worker and motivates others to imitate those traits while desiring for more.

Confront the Process: Leaders confront and pose inquiries to commonly established processes. Hold pioneering methods and measures early on. Learn from your circumstances and emerge as winner.

Encourage a Shared Idea: Support the ideas of the workers with the vision of the institute. Converse this vision so workers accept it. Terror plans are less useful motivators than thoughts. Catch the thoughts of your staffs and ally it with the vision of the company. These are vital abilities to being an efficient leader.

Allow Others to Take Action: Provide workforce the technique, guidance and resources to successfully and proficiently carry out their works and solve issues.

Create the Way Things Want to be Completed: Workforces are more suitable to pursue a leader whose deeds represent what his words articulate.

Promote the Heart inside Your Organisation: People perform on what they are fervent about. Motivate your workforces with your personal successful stories.

Good Communication to be an Excellent Leader: If he has additional leadership skills but if he lacks good communication skills, he can not become an excellent leader anywhere.

Truthfulness: A good leader should be open with both his workers and the management. Another part of his attributes is honesty. Once a leader compromises his or her honesty, it is lost. That is maybe the reason honesty is measured the most estimable feature. Hence the leaders should keep it above all else.

An excellent leader should all the time keep inspiring his group members for good work and must keep up healthy atmosphere. He should provide first priority to protection of employees and observe that they are not oppressed by employers.

Improve your leadership skills by means of these strategies and you will get the status you wish for and deserve as an exact leader. All employers are looking for this type of person in their organisation. It is the person your firm's competition needs on their group. It is the person the management insistently looks for and woes for the next huge challenges or chances you are going to need to consider.

Learning Good Leadership

Learning good leadership will be helpful to become a team leader, supervisor, manager or administrator. Any people who wind up in a leadership role will find themselves struggling to guide others efficiently. In order to become a good leader, your group should be able to respect you. There are many faults made by people who desire to be leaders, and they are frequently committed mistakes as they fail to make out what people need.

Here are some steps you need to follow to get the respect of those you guide:

Encourage: In order to direct or lead your team toward better performance, ensure your workforce feel vested in what they perform. Give them rights of their work so they feel responsible for their effort's achievement. Provide your workforce encouragement to excel.

Interact: Fill your workforce in on the organisation's operation and

possible while changes are happening. Collect workers' comments on workflow. Make workers a part of the decision making method as much as possible. Interaction empowers your workers and makes them more practical in their works. Although you may come across this difficulty sometimes, Interaction permits your workers to rise along with the organisation.

Setting an Example: Show good leadership as a team player. Explain your workers how to work together, distribute resources, collaborate, and perform their best.

Manage: Good leadership has power over work, measures, and work atmosphere. Never possess a liberal managing outlook. Get occupied in routing your team in the way you need them to move.

Be Human: Never try to conceal your faults or exhibit only your strengths, like the conventional uncompromising boss. Confess it while you meet personal restrictions. Reveal good leadership by exhibiting your workers positive ways to handle obstacles, conflict, and problems.

Guide: Guide your subordinates in the whole thing you perform. Explain your workers you are not just their superior but an expert resource for them. Provide workforce training, train argument resolution, and acquire a positive approach toward change.

In order to become a great leader, you must have a balance between dangerous perils and being excessively alert. Improving leadership skills is a long course of action. Some are born with such qualities. They will become leaders much sooner. Moreover leadership is a set of traits as much as a talent. Therefore, it is feasible to learn leadership skills. Begin now and while the opportunity come up you.

Qualities of a Successful Leader

Every one wants to become a leader in life. One cannot become a leader by mere wish; he has to work on that. A person who has these qualities can be a successful leader:

Should be Determined: He must have the power to take decision on right time without depending upon others.

Appreciating Mentality: He must appreciate other people's achievements and also encourage them for further achievements.

Be Active: He must join with others to complete the task and support them at any time for the better performance of the organisation.

Prefer Direct Communication: If he wishes to tell anything to his colleagues or employees, speak directly to them instead of opting paper work.

Authentic and Constant: He must be authentic and constant in his approach, regarding any dealing with others. He should not behave indifferently.

Promote Others: The leader must promote the talented people among the staff to higher positions. He must accept their talent and promote them for their better future.

Think Positively: He must think positively for the better performances of the organisation and also inculcate the positive thinking in his followers.

Be Honest: The leader must be honest in his words and deeds other wise he can not progress in his attempt. No one likes a person who is impure in his acts and thoughts. Try to be honest to become a good leader in your life as well as in your career.

Vision and Motivation: All successful leaders have the skill not just to create an idea but to convey it in a motivating manner. They will see the huge portrait and motivate others to work as one to make it happen.

Excellence: Excellence is one of the important qualities that every leader should have. They have an attitude of constant progress. They seek smarter, better ways of doing things. They are regular learners.

Handle Decisions: Realism is necessary if you wish to become a successful leader. While handle decisions, the top leaders will concentrate on the particulars to decide what is realistic. Visualise you are faced with a badly performing association. You may feel it could be set next day, next week or next month, but the realism may be that it will take months and perhaps years.

Responsibility: The good leaders will accept responsibility to make things happen in an excellent manner. We all can make out how simple it is to blame outer things and we possibly all have done this at some time. If you like to shine as a leader accept liability for making things happen.

Seven Leadership Mistakes

For the greater part of people leadership skills are something that hardly ever comes naturally. But if you pursue some necessary regulations and are ready to realise how to work with people you will have things running much more effortlessly in the company immediately. The mistakes that you must avoid are listed below. Follow these to improve your leadership qualities:

1. Ignoring Employees: Your employees are your business and they must be treated in a good manner. Making any slip up to send this message to employees can be an economic and productivity heave for any business. Employees are people with emotions and feelings and must be informed in several ways how significant they are to the organisation.

2. Failing to Handle Criticism: Just because you are in a headship position does not imply that you unexpectedly become resistant to building the incorrect decisions. At the same time as a leader you must pay attention to positive criticism and make the alteration needed. If an employee thinks to share criticism, the least you can act is take note.

3. Incapable to Assign Responsibilities: This is frequently a problem for small industry mangers. We must believe that our employees can carry out the things we have completed for so long. If they are unable to do the work because a specific talent is required, after that give them the coaching needed or appoint somebody that can. A large part of leadership is about ensuring that things going efficiently and smoothly, and that does not imply running from job to job doing everything ourselves.

4. Realising Everything: Most of the world's famous leaders are people of normal brainpower that do not recognise all there is to make out in their business. They recognise that they can not make out everything and they appoint people that know the whole thing. The success of any industry is in the hands of its employees and the foremost administrators and capitalists of the world all try hard to appoint the best in their business.

5. Procrastination: Postponing something till tomorrow that must be finished today! Frequently procrastination is an outcome of having no preparation or record of priorities. Have a look at goal setting and time management for additional thoughts on how to conquer procrastination.

6. Lack of Focus: Certainly there will be things arise during the day that needs instant action which will divert us from our duty; however we must have a set of priorities to pursue. Performing a little bit of the whole thing gets nothing completed, causing strain and thoughts of being besieged.

7. Scared to Change: The capacity to change in industry is necessary. Changes in expertise, the manner we handle people, the manner we do the business, and in all other part of operating and managing the business. Sticking to old conduct of doing things just because they have all the time been performed that manner is a certain way to go down business. If any feature of the industry can be enhanced then there must be change, even though this means neglecting a poor performing employee or product series that is no longer beneficial.

Tips to Improve Your Leadership Qualities

Leadership is a procedure through which a person can persuade others to accomplish an objective and directs the organisation in an n affective way. Leaders carry out this process by applying their leadership attributes such beliefs, character, knowledge, values, and ethics.

Here are some tips to improve your leadership qualities:

Know Yourself: In order to know yourself, you have to understand your attributes. Seeking self improvement means continually strengthening your attributes. This can be accomplished through self study, formal classes, reflection, and interacting with others.

Be Technically Proficient: As a leader, you must know your job and have a solid familiarity with your employee's task.

Take Responsibility for Your Actions: Search for ways to guide your organisation to new heights .And when things go wrong, they always

corrective action, and move on the next challenge.

Make Sound and Timely Decisions: Use good problem solving, decision making, and planning tools.

Be a Role Model: Be a good model for your employees. They must not only hear what they are expected to do, but also see.

Be Caring: As a good leader you should know about the human nature and the importance of sincerely caring for your workers.

Good Communicator:
them, but also seniors and other key people.

Motivate Your Workers: Help to develop good character traits that will help your worker to carry out their professional responsibilities.

Communication: Ensure that tasks are understood, supervised and accomplished. Communication is the key to this responsibility.

Team Spirit: Although many leaders call their organisation department or section, a team; they are not really teams, they are just a group of people doing their jobs.

Use the full capabilities of your organisation. By developing a team spirit, you will be able to employ your organisation, department or section, to its fullest capabilities.

Maintain a Positive Attitude: No person will respect a crabby or negative person. If you possess positive attitude you will certainly get the attention of your employees. By being positive, you can live a happy life and you can also achieve exciting opportunities and possibilities.

Learn and Improve Yourself

Good leaders always try hard to improve themselves in every possible way. The person, who believes he is brilliant and expert, has lots of things to learn. Don't stop learning as it is essential to improve your knowledge. Be amenable to each person's insights and information from around the world and beyond.

7

Establishing a Successful Teamwork

$\mathcal{M}$ost assignments achieved in the business world are due to successful teamwork. It is common to draw collaborators from various sections and hierarchy stages in dealings before launching a new product or service. In truth, the success of a new venture is obliviously due to the teamwork behind it, so you should put more effort to get a successful and productive team.

Eleven Tips for Preparing a Good Team

1. Decide the intention and objectives of the team. You should note down a business plan which covers the tasks of the team and the hopes superior management has about the team. The entire teammates should keep a copy of this business plan.

2. First select the skilled team members. After declaring the team's objectives, choose the teammates that can carry out each objective. Collaborators should not be restricted to employees; they can include counselors or outworkers with proficiency.

3. Allot a team leader who is skilled and honorable. He or she should challenge the collaborators while giving reference and prop up.

4. Describe every collaborator's duties. Explain the responsibility of every member clearly in a manuscript for teammates to sign. Comprise real objectives and intangibles for example attitude and morals.

5. Carry out team building exercises to generate a unified team. Efficient teams will grow from good relationships, and business teams should form these relationships hastily.

6. Provide each collaborator the resources he requests to carry out his work. This may signify assigning momentary right to normally low ranking staff, for instance augmented access to files or protected parts of the building.

7. Maintain quality all through the procedure. Check your written objectives repeatedly as you struggle to surpass the consumer's expectations.

8. Be receptive of one another's thoughts and views and consider them as something that each one of you can find out and gain from, during the course of work.

9. If a suggestion created by one of your group members does not seem appropriate, explain it in a clear way. It is best that you give his or her suggestion a thought and then create the suitable modification to it. Avoid looking down on your peers' abilities as team leader.

10. Continuously encourage one another to do the tasks successfully. Outstanding groups consist of members who will always help and motivate one another even when times are tough.

11. If you can implement these tips, your collaborators could most possibly be the people whom you would look forward to working with each day, and your task can be finished with a positive mindset or must we say... positive thoughts.

Supervising a Team

skills to direct and control others' aptitudes to the fullest. Profound knowledge regarding the skills and character of each team player assists in entrusting work successfully, encouraging collaborators and forming allegiance among team members.

for your team. Train your team about the goals by speaking clearly regarding their position, tasks and targets.

entrusting some effortless job. Assess their presentation and their skill to achieve the target. Assign work based on the ability and awareness of each person.

the collaborator and pursue through as looked-for in place of micromanaging. A clear perceptive of the necessities gives confidence to the employee to live equal to your anticipation, feel responsible in performing the errands and solve problems actively.

manager who works for his team generates fidelity and encourages the collaborators to go the extra mile for the accomplishment of their team.

team and insert their propositions in your assessment. This participation motivates them to assess their task and role inside the office.

correcting their faults. Be sociable and amicable to them. Recognise and be accepting of their family commitments and troubles.

concerning attendance and timeliness with any positions that want to be filled for instance team leader, goal keeper and minute taker.

task to complete and fix a target, ensure that everybody can make out what you are doing, the hope you have about the teammates and when you want to accomplish your task.

any decision or give suggestions. His main duty is to keep the group on target and handle interruptions and issues within the team.

team to communicate properly, that everybody recognises the task, feels integrated and accepts responsibility for the result.

rolling out your outcome with the entire teammates. Appreciate the group for their excellent work. Try to get feedback from every participant on the things that went well and what could be enhanced in the procedure.

Effective Team Building Skills

Developing team building skills is very much helpful to work successfully with colleagues in your workplace or in personal life. If you have the ability to work in a team or the ability to take initiative always you will have a scope for improvement.

The following ten tips can help you to become a good team player:

1. Always try to compromise. While you work with a team, it is impracticable for you to get their method, so compromise or cooperation is very much required. Never regard it as a blow to your ego, merely a requirement while you improve teamwork skills and utilise it.

2. Never take it personally. While joining with a team, your feelings may get hurt through numb team mates or group

   personal; it must be a normal part of the procedure.

3. Concentrate on the welfare of the task. To improve the teamwork skills, it is very much essential to keep your eye on the work. Focusing your hard works on the achievement of a task takes out the urge to find your own method and assist a team stay on work.

4. Communicate efficiently. If there is no proper communication, all kinds of problems are likely to come up. By speaking in attentive ways and remaining heedful of others' thoughts and motivations, you will be able to work together successfully.

5. Recognise your challenges. If you possess trouble rising teamwork skills, take sufficient time to think about your difficulties. By analysing the difficulties in your way and the reason of your distress, you can work out to conquer them.

6. Join in team building activities. Lots of team building seminars and activities are there to utilise. Find out the time to partake in team building activities to improve teamwork skills.

7. Build up faith with your teammates by spending extra time in an environment of sincerity and honesty. Be reliable to your workers, if you expect the same.

8. Ensure that the team objectives are totally understood and received by every teammate.

9. Ensure there is full clearness in who is liable for what and avoid overlapping authority. For instance, if there is a peril that two teammates will be contending for control in particular part, try to split that part into two different fractions and give each more total control in one of those sections, as per those people's potency and private inclinations.

10. While managing your teams, ensure there are no barriers of communication and you and your teams are kept totally informed.

Working Successfully in Group

Group work or team work is unavoidable in the present day. Often you might have asked to work in groups in school, at office or occasionally while partaking in a volunteer activity. Clear and precise communication is inevitable to work in groups, whether for temporary or permanent jobs.

Try to become acquainted with each other. If you are going to work in a group with others for any extended period of time, use up one or two minutes speaking at the outset of the first get-together. Give proper introduction if you do not know each other.

Allocate positions if the task needs working jointly in a group for a long period of time to attain an exact goal. For example you may assign one person the group head or facilitator and another inscribe or note taker.

Exchange contact details to allow teammates to speak properly outside of planned conferences if the task is long-standing.

Recognise the team's goal. For example, perhaps a lecturer asked you to achieve a task, or your organisation asked you to analyse particular information and submit it. Communicate and record the team's objective to ensure you all choose the chief goal of the team's work.

Split the tasks into parts and allot each person a particular task to assail enduring tasks. Often this will go easier if people volunteer for tasks they akin to perform.

Pay attention to each other and give confidence to each other. Ensure each person in the group is heard and give support while others give a good suggestion or carry out a work successfully.

Handle the conflict straight away if it comes up. Even if hard to handle, divergence or dispute in a team can destabilise the team's goals. As fast as possible, tackle any divergences to keep the teammates concentrated on the ultimate aim.

Speak with your teammates if there is any problem and solve it as soon as possible. While problem arises we must be comfortable to discuss and solve problems. Try to forgive while people commit mistakes.

While strain takes place and tempers flame, take a small break. Refresh yourself, make an apology, and take another attempt at it. Say sorry for distressing your teammates, even though you believe somebody else was initially at fault; the objective is to work as one, not create a legal war over whose wrongdoing were worse. Try to be a mediator.

Essential Team Work Skills

Teamwork is very much required for the successful growth of any organisation. It is one of the most important things you can train your workforce as it affects things like work output, work culture, communication and so on.

Here are some team work skills that the team members should improve to achieve a successful and efficient team.

Listening: Listening skill is essential for developing effective team work. While we talk with other people in our team we will be very concerned about what we should talk next. Obviously we will not listen what other person is talking. This kind of attitude should not be encouraged. Rather than concentrating on what they are speaking we are thinking about what we are going to speak after that, and we will miss most of their points. To avoid this developing listening skill is very much required.

Sacrifi ce: Every team mates must estimate what they are ready to sacrifice and then continue to be willing when the time comes that they are asked to sacrifice it. It could be the whole thing from time, to assets, to status.

Sharing: What one person understands will be the solution to another person's difficulty. We must be ready to share those points even when it will make someone else seem better.

Communication: When there are issues or achievements, profit or lose a team must be ready to communicate properly what went correct and incorrect. It is essential to analyse problems that you face in your task or as a group but it is also significant to analyse your achievements.

Language: It is essential that you must possess an established habit of talking in an inspiring manner. If you are at all degrading or insulting or overbearing it will bring the team to a halt. People will be ready to forfeit, share and confer just not with each teammates implying that the team just turned out to be opponents.

Hard work: Teammates must always be ready to work hard on an individual basis and after that turn that hard work over to the team so that you can make your task meaningful and accomplish a better goal.

Infl uence: Everyone must be motivated to exchange, preserve and then ultimately re-organise their thoughts. You must love your thoughts but collaboration takes individual effort for a collective good that eventually enhances the good quality everyone gets. These skills are a basic list but that will facilitate you begin at this time to be a better team with success. You can not achieve these skills all in one day it takes time, utilise each chance and practice them no doubt you can enhance your team work.

8
Effective Influencing

*I*f you are working in any company or running your own company, influencing is the main leadership skill that you have to build up. Influencing is the skill to affect the verdicts of other people. So how can you make it more effective while it comes to influencing others?

Five Useful Tips

1. Be Apparent on Your Result: In any circumstances where you want to persuade, you are likely to be searching a certain result. It may be a rating, a salary increment, a promotion, a new occupation, extra income or prop up for a suggestion to name a few. Being comprehensible on your result that you want gives the necessary basis for successfully influencing.

2. Look Further Than the Formal Channels: It is very simple to fall into the snare of believing that the formal channels are the only means of influencing. You may have the outlook that the only means to acquire your thoughts or vision across is through the well-known hierarchy. In reality there are some people who voice the views of their superior people. Secretaries or PA's are one instance. There can be somebody in your peer group too who may appear to be the faithful of the superior people. The technique here is to imagine out of the box.

3. Develop Faith: Sustaining your suggestion, submission, thought or plan needs the other person to take some risk. Before any person will take risk, they must recognise that they can belief you. Find out sufficient time and make the attempt to do things to increase faith first. If you have that belief you can request the support.

4. Plan Your Approach: If you are in circumstances where you are trying to persuade without preparation ahead, you are really raising your possibility of failure instead of success. Ask yourself: "What can facilitate you accomplish something?"

After you have answered this question you can begin to imagine regarding the plans you will accept.

All of us have certain circumstances in our life where we want to persuade. Being apparent about what you require, developing faith, looking beyond formal channels, scheduling your approach are just few things that you can try to grow to be more efficient at influencing.

Influencing Skills for Successful Speech

There are many influencing methods that you can utilise when it comes to giving an influential speech. You have to improve your communication skills and, certainly, your influencing skills, to make your viewers trust in you and that viewpoint you are trying to express.

In order to help you with an influential speech, there are lots of tricks you can utilise it to start your opening words. It is almost necessary that you draw the attention of your viewers at your opening statements. You must find out how to catch the viewer's attention and then enhance your speech to keep them involved. The foremost technique that you need to use is a rhetorical query.

Rhetorical Query: A rhetorical query is a query that does not accept any answer but something that gives the viewers to dwell on. Other than, you can utilise a starting statement to catch their concentration. For example, if you throw out some hideous static or numeral that indicates how many people were wounded or injured, you can catch their attention fast.

Techniques of Speech: You must observe the techniques of a speech so that you can display an excellent performance. You should possess the techniques of a speech to help you throughout the speech and also for you to keep you relaxed. You must ensure that the speech you deliver is valuable to your viewer's time and by means of the techniques, you can provide them just that. These are some speaking techniques that you can make use of. Also there are lots of other techniques that you can use in your speech, but you have to form your creditability. You must apply some communication skills even voice modulation, eye contact, and getting to your viewer's thoughts. Certainly, influence skills appear in different works of art.

Persuasion Skills: Influencing and Persuading Others

This is the first of the two articles on effecting change. This time it is external change, which simply denotes change in which you must engage other people to be an active participant, where they must listen to your suggestions in order for that change to take effect. That is, you use your persuasion skills to convince others. Another example is that perhaps you really believe that there should be no war no matter what. In such a case, you would also want to effect external change and be influencing other people.

Set an example. One of the most effective persuasion techniques to persuade others and effect external change is to act in the way that you would like others to act. For instance, if you would like people to work hard, then you yourself should work hard. Not just doing it to display that you work hard, but because you really believe that people should work hard. Similarly, if you feel that people should be courteous, you should speak to people courteously; if you feel people should exercise every morning, you should exercise every morning, and so forth.

If people admire your efforts, or even if they see you do it often enough, they will often imitate what they feel is worthy of imitation.

Children especially are prone to what adults do. You may not know that they are watching, but they definitely can imitate the actions, concerns, and habits that adults have. Even children under five years old can probably be influenced just by observing what others are doing. You need not say a single word and they will absorb it. So, if you would like your children to study hard, you should be setting an example yourself, and not be watching TV everyday.

Hint at the change. If you want to write a story or talk about something, you always have the option of applying persuasion and effecting change. Do so subtly enough that people will not feel that you are giving them a lesson, but do it apparently enough that they understand it. However, do not try to give too many messages at a time. A single message at the end of a story, talk, or speech is really more than enough, as it takes energy and time for people to digest it.

Enlist the help of others when persuading. For some people, no matter what you say, they will ignore it. However, they may believe other people more. Therefore, you may want to enlist the help of someone whom that person trusts. You may get a much better result that way. Especially with regard to a large issue such as preventing war, you will probably need the effort of thousands and thousands of people. In that case, you would probably want to round up as many people as possible.

Set limits on how much persuasion you will do. Effecting external change and persuading others, though difficult, can be one of the most rewarding projects in which you can engage yourself. You reap the rewards directly by seeing how you have improved one aspect of society, since the new behaviour should hopefully make our world a better place. However, you must be careful how often and to whom you try this. You probably would not want to try this on people with whom you are not familiar. Nor would you want to try it on someone who may not follow your advice or good will.

Be patient when trying to persuade and influence others. It would be especially wise to mention a topic only once if it is a very sensitive issue and you get an extremely negative response from the opposite side. However, if the stake is high, you strongly believe in it, and you know the person well, by all means give the persuasion some effort. Sometimes, it is just a matter of time. Wait a bit, and even if it seems that that person did not seem to accept the suggestion, that person may one day decide to follow it after thinking about it. Just remember, though, you may want to examine your own faults before changing other people's faults.

Using Influencing Skills in Your Career Development

When you possess a clear perceptive of what you are contributing to a company, you turn into an empowered person who utilises today's venture to make tomorrow's skills. Using the influence form in your career growth will provide you an additional technique to accomplish your career goals. You must have a career improvement plan with specific objectives with you. Above all you must be well aware of yourself.

There are three important steps towards career growth:

1. Know Yourself: Through developing an exact picture of yourself, you can teach other people what you are able to do. Moreover you can show your potential for further study. This step starts by the influence behaviour of brazenness. Recognise the abilities that you utilise at this time and have used in the earlier period. How can you

2. Recognise Your Choices: Nowadays business or dealings is continuously changing, and mainly the excellent specialists frequently try to influence those changes to attain personal objectives. It is not sufficient just to carry out a huge job at work. Improving various career objectives will help you to explore the future and be prepared for the changes that are going to happen.

the network inside your union and the company where you work. Where will the organisation be two and a half years from at this

3. Realise Your Next Steps: After you have recognised your career objectives, you are prepared to build up your career improvement plan. Your plan must be written and assessable with a particular time period for conclusion. After this plan is organised, talk with your manager or a counselor in the industry. Collecting opinion and prop up for your plan is the important link in accomplishing your objectives.

Making Use of Influence Strategies

After you have finished your career improvement plan, it is time to make them into practical by means of influence skills.

By making a career enhancement plan and energetically including influence strategies in that plan, you apply a powerful technique for your career development. If you are experienced or a fresher in your career, a sturdy, well written plan along with your practice of influence skills will help you achieve your objectives.

Influencing Other People

Influencing people in a dealing situation is about more than just speaking to those people and forcing those people to believe what they are telling. It is about the entire interaction which unites the listener and the narrator in one thinking process.

Systematise Your Views: Make a decision on your goal; what is the topic you need to deal with, why is it significant, and what do you

to be acquainted with your viewers - their backdrops, their position, their inspirations, their qualification, their character, their talents and their skills.

Convey Your Message: Formulate an opener to hold your spectators' attention. Expect all kinds of responses both positive and negative. Try to keep eye contact, speak at their level, smile and maintain your vigor up. You must have confidence in each word you utter. While talking, ensure to advance your views as a discourse and not a monologue.

Find Out Various Responses: Make certain a stable relation between you and your viewers. Ask your viewers for their views, thoughts and queries. Never use negative energies; you don't all the time need to protect your thoughts. Be attentive to non-verbal symbols of distress and divergence, and admit your viewers' questions.

Try to be Work-Oriented

Inquire what you require from your viewers. All the time review your thoughts and decide on the next steps as a group.

Ten Tips for Improving Influencing skills

Here are ten very simple tips regarding improving your influencing skill, you can follow these tips to develop your influencing skills.

1. Try to be more patient, influencing is a course of action.
2. Possess clear ideas about yourself.
3. Listen carefully, to get more knowledge.
4. Be more friendly and accept others ideas and opinions.
5. Make, relation and increase ideas jointly.
6. Show concerned for other people to start common ground.
7. Communicate your views confidently with feelings and facts.
8. Confirm everybody has understood to make sure that people are with you.
9. Be energetic.
10. Particularly organise and plan.

9

Failing to Set Goals

$\mathcal{S}$etting a goal is essential for all kind of achievements in the world. We require goals to show our path. Like a map, goal directs us where we should go and how we can reach there. There are proves that people who have listed their goals seriously accomplish more than the ones who don't. Success is objective. The remaining things are just inserted to give the clear description. Each successful people are aware of goals. They realise what they need and decide each day to accomplish it.

Your talent in goal setting is the main skill for achievement or success. Goals will enlighten your positive thoughts and discharges the thoughts including power for the accomplishment. Without objective, you may float in the tide of life. Your existence will be controlled by the surroundings and others. But with clear objective, your life will be similar to a bullet heads toward the goal without divergence.

Real truth is you have plenty of inborn talents. These talents can give you the opportunity of achievement more than you can dream. What you are possessing at this time is just a small fraction of what you can truly accomplish. It is not significant where you have roots in. The most essential element is where you are leaving. And the location you are going is resolved inside your mind. Real goals will raise your self confidence. It will enhance your ability and effectiveness. It can also enhance your motivation.

If objective is that significant, we should recognise why only some people have goal. There are major four reasons that people don't have goal. These reasons are:

1. They do not recognise the value of goal: First and foremost reason is that people do not understand the value of goal. If you grow up in the family which do not have any objective or if you mingle with the people who never speak about objective or never recognise the importance of objective. It is extremely simple that you mature and become adult without understanding your skill to lay down goal and accomplish it. This skill will have more impact on you more than anything else.

2. They are unaware regarding how to set goals: Second reason is people do not know how to set their goal. The poorer element of it is that they believe they previously have goal but in its place they just have hope or dream. For instance, lots of people think that we would like to be glad or need lots of money or need good relations. All these are not objectives but only dream for them. Goal is entirely dissimilar from wish. It must be evidently written and accurate. You can clarify this to other people and they know what it accurately is. You can calculate it and make out whether you have gained it.

3. They are scared of failure: Failure creates wounds in our mind. It will affect both spiritually and economically. While we fail, we experience the pain and will be more cautious next times not to happen the same thing again. When we have sequence of failures, we begin to produce fear over it. If you have fear in your mind, you automatically stop doing whatever that possibly will result in failing.

4. They are afraid of rejection: If you belong in the same group of people who are unaware of goal setting and do not trust in the power of the objective, the opportunity that you will obtain discarded or laughed at is there. So lots of specialists train us that we simply share our objective with the one who previously have objective of his own and can promote you to follow what you require. You can allow other to view the end result while you accomplish your goal.

You can make use of visualisation to make your goal accomplishment feasible. Visualisation is to view yourself accomplish your objective inside your mind. Perceive it and experience it like it is occurring before you. Visualisation will pull towards you what you wish in your life as per the law of attraction. You can insert attraction acoustic into your visualisation procedure. They are available in the market. Attraction accelerator can be one of your preferences.

Three Successful Goal Setting Strategies

Goal setting is very much essential to your success. Each person knows that to accomplish success that they need in their life, they must lay down some goals. Do you have any idea how to lay down

people do not know how to set successful goals that will drive them into taking instant action.

People fail to achieve their goals as their objectives are not united with what they wish for. They are not using the exact plans to lay down their goals. Goal setting is a simple method. What you want to do is write down in a piece of paper what you wish to achieve and fix it in a place where you can see it frequently. Even though this is a simple method, you may be surprised how people are setting their goals perfectively. Have you ever thought of why some people fail

the main reason people fail to accomplish their goal.

Another reason for the failure is that people will not carry out what they want to do once they have laid down their objective. You must recognise that it is what you execute once you have laid down your goal that will take you to your accomplishment. If you fail to do your work after you have laid down your objectives, nothing is going to happen.

Following are the three goal setting strategies that you want to do once you have laid down your goals. If you try this you can definitely accomplish your goals.

1. Confirm your goals night by night and think about the accomplishment of your goals. You must sink your thought into your subconscious mind and simultaneously, encourage yourself to accomplish it. By doing like this, you are continuously encouraging yourself to carry out your plan.

   come true.

2. Try to take as a minimum three actions which can take you toward your aim each day. Whatever may be your dream you want to work hard to achieve your goal. Goal setting is not a magic stick; you can not accomplish your goal if you are trying hard.

3. Make an open commitment by announcing each person regarding your objective. By doing so, you can achieve your

goals without any difficulty. Sometimes your friends may make fun of you if you tell them about your goal, just ignore it. Twist their negative energy into positive stimulus that pushes you into taking action.

Attaining Your Goals Faster

Goal setting is a significant procedure for personal planning. By laying down objectives on a routine basis you determine what you really wish to accomplish, and then move gradually towards accomplishing these goals. Goal setting will allow you to select where you want to reach in your life. If you have proper goals you can reach there, with out goal or aim our life is meaningless. So in order to lead a meaningful life have some goals in your mind and achieve it.

The following simple tips will help you to set goals in your life and also to achieve it:

1. Try to make every one of your dreams true by recognizing and then concentrating on particular, firm targets for what you require.

   most important interest and position in your life.
3. Lay down your objectives so they are directly united with your life's chore, intention and zeal.
4. Make goals high to enlighten your strength and motivate you to make a start.
5. Jot down the entire goals in detail, assessable point.
6. Perfectly, unreservedly commit to striking each of your objectives.
7. Divide up your objectives with others for shared achievement.
8. Lay down the entire succession of allied daily, weekly and enduring goals; end with opening times and conclusion dates.
9. Spend at least ten minutes each day to visualise how terrific it will seem while your goals are really recognised.
10. Take an action step in the direction of the achievement of one objective each day.
11. Try to set one goal at a time or else it is very hard to fulfill your aspirations.

12. Review your aspiration and motivation. Ensure that you are pursuing objectives for the exact reason.

13. Try to make an open commitment to achieve your objectives. Once you decided to achieve your goal, be committed, and use up the entire time to work on your task. Maintain a record of your growth.

14. Get motivation for attaining your goals. Find any person who has achieved their goals in their life to get a motivation out of them.

15. Determination and fortitude are very essential to get your goals. With strong determination work on your goals and achieve it. With out goals life is meaningless.

If you are able to follow these guidelines, they can give you the drive to succeed in your goals and in life as well. Goal setting process can be clichīd but if you pursue these tips to accomplish it, you can attain the goals in your life you desired.

Techniques for Setting Personal Goals

Goal setting very much required for personal planning. By setting goals you can decide what you want to accomplish and after that you can move gradually towards accomplishing these goals. Goal setting process will help you to decide where you want to reach in future. By setting smart, clearly defined goals, you can calculate and rejoice in the attainment of those objectives. When you set goals you can improve your confidence and also can realise your abilities.

Goals are laid down on a number of different levels: At first you determine what you really wish to do with your life and what goals you want to accomplish. Second, you break these down into the smaller targets. Finally once you have your plan; you start working towards achieving it.

Here are some helpful techniques for you:

Set Your Goals: The first step in setting personal goals is to consider what you want to achieve in your life, as setting life time goals gives you the overall perspective that shapes all other aspects of your decision making. To give a broad, balanced coverage of all important areas in your life, try to set goals in some or all of the following categories:

Artistic:

Attitude:

so, set a goal to develop your conduct or get a solution to the problem.

Career:

Education:

What kind of knowledge and abilities will you want to attain

Family:

Financial:

Physical: Are there any athletic goals you want to achieve, or

Pleasure:

make sure that some of your life is for you

Public service: Do you wish to create the world a better place

Evaluate the Goals

Once you have determined your objectives in these groups, allocate a main concern to them from A to Z. Then evaluate the objectives and re-priorities until you are pleased that they reproduce the figure of the life that you crave to direct. Moreover make sure that the objectives that you have laid down are the objectives that you wish to accomplish, not what your parents, partner, relatives, or managers want to them to be.

Accomplish Your Goals

After you have laid down your goals, set a twenty-five years plan of smaller goals that you must complete if you are to arrive at your lifetime plan. Then set a five-year plan, one-year plan, six-month plan and one-month plan of progressively smaller goals that you must reach to attain your lifetime goals. Each of these should be based on the previous plan.

Lastly lay down a daily to-do list of things that you must do today to work towards your goals. At an early period these objectives may be to read books and collect information on the accomplishment of your objectives. This will facilitate you to develop the value and practicality of your goal setting. In the closing stages evaluate your plans, and ensure that they fit the manner in which you feel like to live your life. After you have determined your primary set of plan, maintain the procedure going by analysing and updating your to-do list on a daily basis. Intermittently evaluate the longer term plans, and alter them to reproduce your varying priorities and experience.

10

Managing Your Time

$\mathcal{I}$n today's fast growing world the influence of computer and Internet has made our life faster and easier. Developing time management skill is very much required in our busy life otherwise it is very difficult to move our life forward. Here are some helpful tips for you to mange your time.

Tips to Manage Your Time

- Make a plan or to-do list. Set down deadlines for achieving particular tasks.
- Decide to undertake complicated tasks at the times of day while you are most attentive.
- Make some personal time by getting up half an hour before or going to bed half an hour later than usual; plan a weekly date with your partner, or assemble to have lunch with associates.
- Prioritise what you want to achieve. According to that make a schedule and work out to achieve your goals.
- Assign as many tasks as you can. Hand out tasks to subordinates at work, employ your kids to help with household works, appoint a gardener to keep up your home turf.
- Train yourself to say no to unnecessary demands on your time. Never volunteer for a team if you don't have sufficient time, and refuse invitations to any programs if you do not have time to participate.
- Conquer procrastination.
- Avoid fastidiousness. Never waste time obsessively perfecting a mission while you could better use up the time on something else.
- Try to reduce disruptions by making strong borders. It is correct that disruptions to your daily work can and will take place, and to certain extend they are beyond your control. But, you most likely have more control than you believe. Rather than blaming others and getting annoyed with them for disrupting you, make strong borders with your colleagues wherever necessary.

others and entrust some works to them. This will help you to get some extra time and you can relax yourself.

not enough for us to complete our daily tasks because we do not know how to manage the time effectively. Make sure that you are utilising the entire time without wasting, then you can carry out your work within a fixed time. To improve your time management skill it is necessary to fix a target and try hard to complete your work within a fixed target. If so, you can complete your tasks and achieve your target as well.

Developing Your Time Management Skills

Time management is an essential skill to build up in your daily life. Time management is very much required in business, where time is money. If you realise that you are spending lots of your time rather than concentrating on the things that you really need to get done, this is the right time to improve your time management skill. If you can manage your time in a proper manner it not only improves your earning but improves your interest towards work also.

Here are five tips to help you in developing your time management skills:

1. Prepare lists of the things that you really crave to achieve for the week. Note them down in a paper or put them in your task calendar. Try to place them in a visible area so that it can remind you about the things that you need to do. By doing like this you can finish your task within the short time period with out getting delay. Preparing such lists will help you to improve your time management skill.

    dates for all these tasks this will help you to reorganize them in order of priority. Assigning this kind of target will help you to carry out your work within the fixed time period. If possible, avoid working at the last moment it makes more stress and you will not get any perfection to your work. So avoid such situations.

3. Try to bar the time on your calendar and utilise this time to carry out your personal work. By doing like this you are offering yourself a chance to get your work done. More over you can stop other people from booking your precious time.

4. Ask yourself some questions. Try to ask questions regarding the importance of the new things that you immediately find yourself being asked to work up. It seems easy, yet too often these queries linger unasked and precious time is used up on things of lesser worth.

5. Observe how you are spending your days, weeks, months, etc. If you observe like this, you will get the idea about where most of your valuable moments are used up. Try to find ways to develop your output and proficiency. If so next time you can use up your time much more carefully.

Time Management-To-Do Lists

A 'To-Do List' is a list of everyday jobs that you want to complete. It combines all the works that you must do into one place. You can categorise these works in the order of importance. This permits you to undertake the most significant ones at first.

To-do lists are very much required while you have to do lots of different works, or else when you have made many commitments. If you feel that you are repeatedly trapped because you have forgotten to carry out something, then you want to prepare a to-do list.

As to-do lists are very simple, they are also really prominent, both as a way of arranging yourself and as a method of reducing strain. Frequently problems may appear overpowering or you may have huge amount of demands on your time. This may leave you feeling out of control, and overloaded with job.

It is very easy to prepare to-do-list. Note down the works that face you, and if you feel it as hefty, make them down into their constituent rudiments. If you fell still large, split them again. Continue this until you have scheduled all things that you want to-do. If too many tasks have a higher priority, go through the chart again and downgrade the insignificant ones. Once you completed this, redraft the list in priority order. You will then get an accurate plan that you can utilise to eradicate the troubles you come across.

You can undertake this in order of importance. This permits you to divide significant jobs from the time-consuming insignificant ones.

Besides your daily to-do list, maintain a constant list of tasks that you want to achieve, Revise this list once in a week. Plan things with satisfaction, giving time for sudden delays or misfortunes; avoid an intolerably rigid schedule.

Various people utilise to-do lists in dissimilar ways in different circumstances: if you are in a sales-type position, better method of encouraging yourself is to maintain your list comparatively small and plan to do it daily. In an operational position, or else if works are hefty or rely on more people, then it will be better to prepare one list and 'chip away' at it. It may be that you take insignificant works from one to-do list to the next. Sometimes you can not finish some priority works for several months then set a target for them and increase their priority.

Tips for Improving Your Time Management Skills

Follow the given tips to improve your time management skill:

creative.

down in a paper.

minutes.

than 30 minutes.

do-list and follow that list to accomplish your goals.

personal work .By doing so you are allowing yourself an opportunity to get your things done.

track everything that you need to achieve.

can jot down your thoughts and plans in it.

they take place

someone else.

you are completed.

assignment.

worker.

11

Self Motivation

*I*mproving your motivation skill is a kind of art. It involves lots of practice to make it perfect. As we think it is not so difficult to develop the motivation skill. Here are some points to help you out to develop your motivation skill. Set a plan in your mind and try hard to achieve it.

Five Useful Tips for Self Motivation

1. Lay down a Plan: Planning is the most important thing. Planning is very much required for every field. Set a goal in your mind and then plan your actions to achieve your goals. Proper planning can help you to achieve your goal. If you have goal or purpose in your mind, definitely you will try hard for that, no doubt you will motivate yourself to achieve your goals. In this manner you can develop your motivation skill. Once you have laid down a goal, break it into smaller ones this will help you to assess how much you have advanced in your goal setting.

2. Dedicate Yourself to Your Aims: An outlook makes lot of disparity when it comes to self motivation. There is a dissimilarity between saying "I will try my level best to attain my objectives" and "I will attain my objectives". You should completely dedicate yourself to achieve your objectives .This will bring lots of changes to your motivation as your sub-conscious records this as an 'order'. It will modify the entire attitude and provide you the necessary motivation whenever you require it.

3. Take Action: After you have laid down your goals and dedicated yourself to goals, you have to start taking action. Actual reason is that while the mind perceives things happening around it, it provides you the essential self motivation drive.

4. Take Motivation 'Food': When you take some actions related to your goals you should feed your mind with some motivation food. Try to challenge yourself and always imagine that you have achieved your goals. This will provide you positive energy and thus you can motivate yourself. In order to keep yourself motivated you can read the successful stories of famous people. This will motivate you to do better in your life. Following their path you can get succeed in your personal life.

5. Evaluate Your Performance: In the beginning you had laid down some goals. In order to acquire additional motivation repeatedly evaluate your performance against your objectives. Don't be discouraged if you didn't get the expected output. You just want to do more hard work till you achieve your goal.

Sources of Motivation

We must have a strong motivation to achieve success in any field. Suppose you want to build a big house, let that house be your motivation. If you wish for a good career, let that career with good salary be your motivation. Or maybe you need to have more leisure time with your family, let that be your motivation. Each person wants a nudge to push them forward. Motivation acts as a driving force .If you want to achieve anything in your life you require a driving force or else you cannot achieve anything in your life. Motivation is driving force. If you have motivation you can easily achieve your life goals.

Certainly, motivation alone is not sufficient to be victorious; you also require knowledge, abilities, perseverance, insistence and more highly focused and colossal actions. But, the main obstruction to being successful is the lack of motivation.

To boost your odds and accomplish success sooner; never lose sight of success. All the time concentrate on your goals and imagine that you are going to acquire what you need in your life in the future. It is not expectation and it is not a desire either. It has got to be a truth. While you think success is not just an alternative but a truth, the quicker you will accomplish the success you crave.

For instance, if a sportsperson wants to achieve his medal; that person will be doing thorough practice each single day and dreaming himself wearing the gold medal. It will be the main aim of all the athletes. It motivates them to progress steadfastly towards his goal.

Further source for motivation is to encircle yourself with positive minded people. Irrespective of how optimistic or motivated you are, you are still vulnerable to pessimistic influences. By surrounding yourself with winning people, they not only can facilitate to inspire you but also share positive belief and skill. This

from pessimistic people.

Reading self development and self motivation book will help you to get motivation. Take a notebook, cut and fix the photos of people or things there which can remind you about your objectives. This will inspire you each time you turn over the pages in your notebook.

Recite the positive words such as: "I have the wish and inner force to accomplish my objectives". Say again this statement frequently, with belief and strong mind-set.

Motivation is a driving force that takes you towards achievement and success in all realms of life. Motivate yourself to achieve your goals and success.

Self Motivation Tips

No one has the capability to motivate or inspire themselves better then you can motivate yourself that is why it is called self motivation. The most important self motivation tip is accepting that self motivation originate from ourselves, not from external source. It is not an external process. Here are some useful self motivation tips:

Build up a Plan: In order to motivate yourself, you should make out what you need to attain. You can build up a short and long term plan. If you lay down higher objectives that can not be achievable you may be destined for failure and that is not very inspiring. After you have recognised your goals note them down in a notepad or paper and place it where it is observable to you always and read it daily. All the time speak as if your objectives are previously achieved and imagine what it will be like while all your objectives are recognised. Speak about your objectives and thoughts until you feel they are genuine.

Prevent Procrastination: Procrastination is a big motivation destroyer. Set time limitations on the assignment you are doing. Be very precise with your time restrictions. The thought that there is a time limit will inspire or motivate you to complete your project. Employ this self motivation tip on whatever thing you want to get done, whether it is a tiny or big task. Beware though and make your time limit pragmatic, it is not good to make needless strain from an objective you lay down for yourself.

Admire Yourself: Each person likes to be admired while they achieve something in their life. Therefore admire or praise yourself if you conclude a task within the time limit you had given. Never wallow in your own conceit evermore. All the time set new objectives while one is achieved. Successful people constantly seek new methods to develop themselves and their lives.

Avoid being a Perfectionist: Try to get work achievement and not perfection. Trying for aptness or perfection will direct to procrastination. There is a propensity for you not to carry out the work since you have the thought that you will never execute an ideal work. Admit the thing that no one is perfect and this will certainly encourage you.

Enjoy Yourself: House-based works will be extremely difficult task; hence a sense of humour is an important element in your success recipe. Don't take yourself or your work too gravely. Enjoy yourself when you carry out your work as it keeps you energetic and motivated. Moreover staying energetic and motivated helps you maintain your strain levels under control.

Improving Motivation skills

For some people inspiring or motivating themselves will be a very tough job. For such people it is like a folk story where the whole thing is fabulous and good but which they are unable to achieve. But it is not so difficult, as we think.

Using these motivation tips one can improve the motivation skills:

Recognise Yourself : Recognising your inner self is the most important thing you want to do to improve your motivation skill. Motivation is closely related with your self re-organisation. The more you understand yourself, the easier it will be to motivate you. Analyse yourself, sit and

answered properly to know about you. This self understanding will help you to motivate yourself.

Accept Responsibility: Never blame others for your incapability and lack of motivation remember it is merely a waste of time. People who continuously blame their employer for their lack of motivation on their work will certainly stay irritated and fail in their effort. Do not allow others' deeds and words have an impact on your inspiration.

Think Positively: Positive thinking has an important role in self motivation. Positive thinking always energises your innersole and there by you get self motivation. You must improve your positive thinking if you really want to get self motivation. So start thinking positively. Pessimism, terror and anxiety will never help you to move ahead. Positive thinking is the only one important thing that can build or smash your motivation skill.

Avoid Comparison: Do not compare yourself with others. Comparison will never help you to get motivated instead it prevents your growth. If you compare yourself with others it is equal to insult your self image. Concentrate on being the greatest that you can be and permit other people to act the similar thing.

Set a Goal in Your Mind: Goal setting will definitely help you to improve your motivation skill. If you have some goals in your mind, you will really struggle to achieve it. In order to achieve your goals you have to motivate yourself, so this goal setting will help you to improve your motivation skill. The most important thing regarding goal is that it provides you a proper way to work in and it makes you liable to yourself. By setting goals one can improve their motivation skill.

Steps to Improve Your Motivational Skills

Motivation skills are very much required if we need success, achievement, and strength all through our life. We possibly will benefit from talented motivational orators, books, and classes. But if we want to go ahead and make development in attaining our objectives we should build up our own personal skills for staying motivated.

Motivational skills are skills that can be learned and enhanced with effort and time. We never reach a point where we can stop sharpening these self motivation skills. When we become more talented we can go ahead more rapidly and attain even higher objectives.

Step-1: The foremost thing you want to do to achieve some self motivation skills is take action. If you are really motivated to perform something chances are it will get completed. All of us are culpable for at least once in our lives asserting that we were planning to perform something tomorrow, but that is not taking action that is postponing. Learn self motivation skills to help out you attain your objectives sooner. The initial step includes arranging a list of things that you want to execute the next day before you go to bed stressing on the things that totally must be completed.

Step-2: The next step is while you wake up in the dawn; the foremost thing you carry out is have a look at your list and create a note of the things that must be supported. Another thing that you should do is memorize the earlier period and remember the things that inspired you. It is fine idea to utilise these motivators to facilitate you complete your job.

Step-3: The next thing is to admire yourself after the completion of each work. You should concentrate on the work at hand with out allowing yourself get diverted. Easy things like regularly being on the telephone or viewing television will gradually but certainly turn you away from your task. While you are completed, all the time rejoice the conclusion of your works.

Step-4:
easily attain the level of motivation you need at whatever time you wish. Once you get self motivation, nothing can stop you from attaining your goals.

While you rehearse these motivational skills, make it a habit to use it daily, you are improving yourself to be a motivated man. Like any other things, motivation is a product out your behaviour. Before you make out it, you can analyse yourself having motivation in anything you perform.

12

Basics of
Conflict Management

Conflict is when two or more values, perspectives and opinions are contradictory in nature and haven't been aligned or agreed about yet. Conflict is:

- within yourself when you're not living according to your values;
- when your values and perspectives are threatened;
- discomfort from fear of the unknown or from lack of fulfillment.

Conflict is inevitable and often good, for example, in a game good teams always go through a "form, storm, norm and perform" period. Getting the most out of diversity means often-contradictory values, perspectives and opinions.

Conflicts can Reveal Reality

- It helps to raise and address problems.
- It energises work to be on the most appropriate issues.
- It helps people "be real", for example, it motivates them to participate.
- It helps people learn how to recognise and benefit from their differences.

Conflict is not the same as discomfort. The conflict isn't the problem - it is when conflict is poorly managed that is the problem.

Conflict is a problem when it hampers productivity; lowers morale; causes more and continued conflicts or causes inappropriate behaviours.

Managerial Actions that Cause Workplace Conflicts

Poor Communication

a. Employees experience continuing surprises, they are not informed of new decisions, programs, etc.

b. Employees don't understand reasons for decisions. They are not involved in decision-making.

c. As a result, employees trust the "rumor mill" more than management.

The Alignment

a. Disagreement about "who does what".

b. Stress from working with inadequate resources.

Confl icting Values among Managers and Employees

a. Strong personal natures don't match.

b. We often don't like in others what we don't like in ourselves.

Leadership Problems

a. Avoiding conflict, "passing the buck" with little follow-through on decisions.

b. Employees see the same continued issues in the workplace.

c. Supervisors don't understand the jobs of their subordinates.

Building Relationships with All Subordinates

a. Meet at least once a month alone with them in office.

b. Ask about accomplishments, challenges and issues.

Getting Regular, Written Status Reports

a. About accomplishments.

b. Currents issues and needs from management.

c. Plans for the upcoming period.

Conducting Basic Training

a. Interpersonal communications.

b. Conflict management.

c. Delegation.

Employees' Input

a. Have employees write procedures when possible and appropriate.

b. Get employees' review of the procedures.

c. Distribute the procedures.

d. Train employees about the procedures.

e. Regularly hold management meetings, monthly or bimonthly, to communicate new initiatives and status of current programs.

f. Consider an anonymous suggestion box in which employees can provide suggestions.

Ways to Deal with Conflict

There is no one best way to deal with conflict. It depends on the current situation. Here are the major ways that people use to deal with conflict:

By Avoiding it:

Pretend it is not there or ignore it. Use it when it simply is not worth the effort to argue. Usually this approach tends to worsen the conflict over time.

Accommodating it:

Give in to others, sometimes to the extent that you compromise yourself. Use this approach very sparingly and infrequently, for example, in situations when you know that you will have another more useful approach in the very near future. Usually this approach tends to worsen the conflict over time, and causes conflicts within yourself.

Competing:

Work to get your way, rather than clarifying and addressing the issue. Competitors love accommodators. Use when you have a very strong conviction about your position.

Compromising:

Enjoy mutual give-and-take. Use when the goal is to get past the issue and move on.

Collaborating:

Focus on working together. Use when the goal is to meet as many current needs as possible by using mutual resources. This approach sometimes raises new mutual needs. Use when the goal is to cultivate ownership and commitment.

Ways to Manage a Conflict Within Yourself

It's often in the trying that we find solace, not in getting the best solution. The following steps will help you in this regard:

1. **Name the confl ict, or identify the issue, including what you want that you aren't getting:**

the conflict in 5 sentences or less.

2. Get perspective by discussing the issue with your friend or by putting it down in writing and consider these aspects:

3. Pick at least one thing you can do about the confl ict:

alternative that will not hurt, or be least hurtful, to yourself and others.

4. Wait for the cooling off period:

This gives you a cooling off period.

see no clear improvement.

To Manage a Conflict with Other Person

1. **Know what you don't like about yourself, early on in your career:** We often don't like in others what we don't want to see in ourselves.

others.

2. **Manage yourself:** If you and/or the other person are getting heated up, then manage yourself to stay calm by any of these.

- this can be very effective!

3. Move the discussion to a private area, if possible:

4. Give the other person time to vent:

5.Verify that you're accurately hearing each other:

you rephrase what you are hearing from them to ensure you are hearing correctly.

"why" questions - those questions often make people feel defensive.

6. Repeat the above step, this time for them to verify that they are hearing you: When you present your position do any of the following things.

7. Work the issue, not the person: When they are convinced that you understand them then ask these things..

to complain again.

8. If possible, identify at least one action that can be done by one or both of you:

9. Thank the person for working with you.

10. If the situation remains a confl ict, then resort to any of these methods:

and procedures in the workplace and if so, present the issue to your supervisor.

13

Change Management

$\mathcal{A}$t the heart of the change management lies the change problem, that is, some future state to be realised; some current state to be left behind; and some structured, organised process for getting from the one to the other. The change problem might be large or small in scope and scale, and it might focus on individuals or groups or one or more divisions or departments or the entire organisation.

The Change Problem

At a conceptual level, the change problem is a matter of moving from one state (A) to another state (B). Moving from A to B is typically accomplished as a result of setting up and achieving three types of goals: transform, reduce, and apply.

- Transform goals are concerned with identifying differences between the two states.
- Reduce goals are concerned with determining ways of eliminating these differences.
- Apply goals are concerned with putting into play operators that actually effect the elimination of these differences.

As the goal types suggest, the analysis of a change problem will at various times focus on defining the outcomes of the change effort, on identifying the changes necessary to produce these outcomes, and on finding and implementing ways and means of making the required changes. In simpler terms, the change problem can be treated as smaller problems having to do with the how, what, and why of change.

Change as a "How" Problem: The change problem is often expressed, at least initially, in the form of a "how" question. How do we get people to be more open, to assume more responsibility, to be more creative? How do we introduce self-managed teams in Department W? How do we change over from System X to System Y in Division Z? How do we move from a mainframe-centered computing environment to one that accommodates and integrates PCs? How do we get this organisation to be more innovative, competitive, or productive? How do we raise more effective barriers

In short, the initial formulation of a change problem is means-centered, with the goal state more or less implied. There is a reason why the initial statement of a problem is so often means-centered and we will touch on it later. For now, let's examine the other two ways in which the problem might be formulated — as "what" or as "why" questions.

Change as a "What" Problem: As was pointed out in the preceding section, to frame the change effort in the form of "how" questions is to focus the effort on means. Diagnosis is assumed or not performed at all. Consequently, the ends sought are not discussed. This might or might not be problematic. To focus on ends requires the posing of

Change as a "Why" Problem: Ends and means are relative notions, not absolutes; that is, something is an end or a means only in relation to something else. Thus, chains and networks of ends-means relationships often have to be traced out before one finds the "true" ends of a change effort. In this regard the "why" questions prove extremely useful. Consider the following imaginary dialogues with "why" questions as an example of tracing out ends-means relationships:

1. **Why do people need to be more creative?**
   I'll tell you why! Because we have to change the way we do things and we need ideas about how to do that.
2. **Why do we have to change the way we do things?**
   Because they cost too much and take too long.
3. **Why do they cost too much?**
   Because we pay higher wages than any of our competitors.
4. **Why do we pay higher wages than our competitors?**
   Because our productivity used to be higher, too, but now it's not.
5. **Eureka! The true aim is to improve productivity!**
   No it isn't; keep going.

6. **Why does productivity need to be improved?**
   To increase profits.

7. **Why do profits need to be increased?**
   To improve earnings per share.

8. **Why do earnings per share need to be improved?**
   To attract additional capital.

9. **Why is additional capital needed?**
   We need to fund research aimed at developing the next generation of products.

10. **Why do we need a new generation of products?**
    Because our competitors are rolling them out faster than we are and gobbling up market share.

11. **Oh, so that's why we need to reduce cycle times.**

To ask "why" questions is to get at the ultimate purpose of the functions and to open the doors to find the new and better ways

purposes of people, but that's a different matter altogether, a "political" matter and one we'll not go into in this space.

Thirteen Useful Tips to Manage Change

The honest answer is that you manage it pretty much the same way you'd manage anything else of a turbulent, messy, chaotic nature, that is, you don't really manage it, you grapple with it. It's more a matter of leadership ability than management skill.

1. The first thing to do is jump in. You can't do anything about it from the outside.

2. A clear sense of mission or purpose is essential. The simpler

   is a whole lot more meaningful than "Respond to market needs with a range of products and services that have been carefully designed and developed to compare so favorably in our customers' eyes with the products and services offered by our competitors that the majority of buying decisions will be made in our favor."

3. Build a team. "Lone wolves" have their uses, but managing change isn't one of them. On the other hand, the right kind of lone wolf makes an excellent temporary team leader.

4. Maintain a flat organisational team structure and rely on minimal and informal reporting requirements.

5. Pick people with relevant skills and high energy levels. You'll need both.

6. Toss out the rulebook. Change, by definition, calls for a configured response, not adherence to prefigured routines.

7. Shift to an action-feedback model. Plan and act in short intervals. Do your analysis on the fly. No lengthy up-front studies, please. Remember the hare and the tortoise.

8. Set flexible priorities. You must have the ability to drop what you're doing and tend to something more important.

9. Treat everything as a temporary measure. Don't "lock in" until the last minute, and then insist on the right to change your mind.

10. Ask for volunteers. You'll be surprised at who shows up. You'll be pleasantly surprised by what they can do.

11. Find a good "straw boss" or team leader and stay out of his or her way.

12. Give the team members whatever they ask for - except authority. They will generally ask only for what they really need in the way of resources. If they start asking for authority, that's a signal they're headed toward some kind of power-based confrontation and that spells trouble. Nip it in the bud!

13. Concentrate dispersed knowledge. Start and maintain an issues logbook. Let anyone go anywhere and talk to anyone

spaced, and easily hurdled. Initially, if things look chaotic, relax - they are.

Remember, the task of change management is to bring order to a messy situation, not pretend that it's already well organised and disciplined.

14

Solving Disputes at Workplace

$\mathcal{A}$re you a victim of organisational conspiracy? Hostility in the office can be traumatic and counterproductive for each person occupied. Approach the individual with whom you are in dispute and solve the condition. If you have any problem in your workplace there are lots of methods, both informal and formal, that can help to solve the problems. Before searching a solution to the problem you must realise what the real problem is and ensure that this is not a simple faults or misinterpretation.

Simple Tips

Here are some simple tips to lessen awkwardness in the workplace. Come to a decision whether you need to deal with the person who is troubling you.

- Approach the person peacefully, graciously and wisely. Concentrate on the condition and specifics, avoiding rumor and personal harassment.

- Beware not to express resentment in your attitude, body movements or voice. Be confident without being hostile.

- Pay attention to the other person carefully: What he or she is trying to speak? Be certain you are aware of her or his position.

- Invite others to discuss the issues. A hasty communication at your desk between telephone conversation and emails will not solve the problems. You require an uninterepted atmosphere and time to solve the problems.

- Show interest in what he or she is talking. You can admit his or her thoughts without necessarily approving or presenting. Speaking, "I realise that you think this manner. Here is how I think..." admits both positions.

- Make an apology for your role in the dispute. Generally everybody involved has done something to make and continue the disputes. Keep in mind: You are not admitting the whole faults, you are accepting liability for your contribution to the circumstances.

it is worth it to you to solve the dispute. This will be tough while some people feel it very simple   to appreciate and praise a person they oppose strongly with but it is a great way to go forward.

to set an objective so both parties can identify the result they are waiting for. This makes getting the result a lot more likely.

advices. Try to be more flexible.

badly threatens your effort, other than keep away from whining.

15

Meeting Your Deadlines

$\mathcal{S}$ome people find it very difficulty to achieve their target in their work. This is due to the lack of proper time management.

Achieving Targets

Here are nine useful guidelines for you to help you with achieving your targets:

1. Be aware of the task entrusted on you.

2. Recognise when your task must be finished, after that reckon how much time you need to complete it. Depending on the task, this can be days, weeks or months.

3. Consider what possibly will detour you. The more time critical the project, the more significant it is that you are practical regarding what else is on your plate.

4. Divide the huge tasks into smaller ones. For instance, you can break up marriage scheduling into buying a costume, finding a party locality, appointing a caterer and so forth .In order to make an exact plan for the task, calculate how much time you take to complete every task, making certain to make in time for unexpected conditions or hindrances.

5. Describe every task, and plan starting and ending dates for every task. Ensure you repeatedly assess how reasonable your time frame is.

6. Build a check list and plan for every task. Make use of some method doesn't matter what method works for you to stay on path: every day join up with your plan, a reminder or an alarm on your digital diary.

7. Seek help from trustworthy friends or coworkers. You are not only saving the time but also allowing others on your group while they donate to the task. Hand over the entire tasks excluding those that only you can get completed. Plan regular conference with your group to ensure tasks remain on plan and within finances.

8. Slash corners where you can without affecting the overall value. Reassess your target and keep combining tasks and cutting additional task until you can get the work completed.

9. Be careful to evaluate the circumstances with a peaceful mind when you follow. Make out certain jobs that may be delaying the tasks or are just not going to get completed in due course. If probable, appoint somebody to assist you.

Draw together your group once the deadline has been met. Talk about the task and decide if objectives were met, how the method could have been enhanced and how teammates executed. Demand sincere comment from each person with the perceptive that your final craving is enhanced presentation on the next target

16

Achieving Negotiation Skills

$\mathcal{W}$e are negotiating whenever we are involved in a transaction, it is happening everyday. If you need a successful career and personal life, it is better to improve your negotiation skill. Negotiation skills are very much required for working out task details, getting resources, buying apparatus, negotiating agreement, and gaining a new career or promotion.

Useful Tips

1. Make inquiries earlier than you begin your negotiation; this will get you more equipped to negotiate.
2. Keep a positive outlook; it will work in your favor most times. Make propositions rather than challenging, this will be more effectual.
3. It is always better to follow your goals. Recognise your goals; lay down goals that are in your confines. Remark upon what you have in mind and how much you are agreeable to negotiate.
4. If you are asking for an increment, ensure that you possess reports of what other people, in similar situation are making.
5. Try to be frank rather than guarded.
6. Never gets angry while you lose control or el se you will make wrong decision. It every so often become disturbed, but keeps concentrating on your objectives.
7. Be aware of the other person's worries and requirements, and make a healthy relationship with the person with whom you are negotiating.
8. The ultimate result of the negotiation will rely on your performance. Be ready to listen, successful listeners can easily pick up information, which are significant.
9. Discuss shared objectives and benefits instead of seeing the other party as the opponent.
10. Keep in mind your goal to attain agreement. This may imply letting go of some respected positions.
11. Never show aggression on the other party. Stay away from emotion. Be cool and practical.

12. Avoid making any compromise before discussing it with your coworkers.
13. People are ready to make more compromises if they feel safe. Do not be aggressive.
14. Ensure that you carry your list of objectives with you, so that you can keep yourself in check.
15. Be optimistic, this will enhance your self-confidence.
16. Negotiation is time consuming and can be emotional sometimes.

Once you achieve fundamental negotiation skills, you can make use of them in various situations. Negotiation skills will always help you to create healthy relationships with person with whom you are negotiating. Negotiation skill helps to make a good team work. Nowadays team work is very common in all workplace. So it is very much required to improve your negotiation.

Negotiating in a Better Way

Negotiation is an essential thing, that every one of us applies at several times, at various stages of our life, to accomplish different objectives. In order to negotiate successfully one should do a good research on the self strength and weaknesses.

The following tips will help you to negotiate in a better way:

make you happy and work hard to achieve it.

planning opportunity.

all, their interests are fulfilled. You can ask unlimited queries to understand these requirements and to recognise their situation.

other person's incentives.

problems. Never harass the person. This will not be favorable to working with them. Be polite and sensitive.

particularly if they have to convince others to facilitate you. As a companion, they will be able to advertise your thoughts and contract.

Get ready to clarify point and substantiate to that person why they must admit your offer.

try again. Slow but stable progress generates momentum that can guide to harmony.

to walk off or else do you have to perform it at this time.

find out where your interests shared with others, where they are in conflict and find a suitable outcome.

body language and essential modifications in behaviour.

require.

The first and foremost step to get good outcome is changing the manner you think about negotiation. Following a method or plan is good, but realising the approach of the people with whom you are making negotiation, and altering your style to converse more efficiently will be the key to achievement. Developing a strategy earlier regarding real negotiation will improve the confidence level and also guide to a better output.

Winning the Negotiations

In today's rapid growing world good negotiation skill is very much required. Once you have recognised what you require, you can make use of your skills to attain it. An effective negotiation means that both parties will get what they need during a series of useful deliberations.

Practice systematically for the negotiation before you start negotiating. You should ensure that you know what main points you need to present during the negotiation prior to the negotiation. Sit down and dwell on the opinions your opponent is going to formulate. Figure out conflicts to all of the opinions before you start the negotiation.

Bear in mind that negotiation is not a winning and losing game, it is only a win-win game In order to win negotiation, you must train to lower your status and primary position.

In whichever negotiation method, never be the one offering the last contract. Allow your opponent presents his last deal, and you determine whether you admit the contract or not.

Make use of the tips given below to win any type of negotiation that you come across:

> your opponent will think that something you suggest is not precious or valuable.

> by ensuring that you have a positive outlook regarding the negotiations. Start your negotiation believing that you will acquire what you wish finally. Practice some recreation exercises and concentrate on the outcome that you require, after that, go out and acquire it.

> using technical terms as it confuses your adversary. This will cause them to turn into cynical and they become more rigid throughout the negotiation.

> change you into your next shtick. This will make you to misinterpret something. Be an energetic listener by listening with your ears, eyes and brain.

> Don't be scared of looking stupid by asking questions. You must ensure that you recognise what they are speaking so you can acquire what you need from the negotiation.

Be more flexible throughout the negotiation. The end result of a negotiation is that it be a win-win state. If a negotiation is completed exactly, then both parties must obtain what they require at last. On the other hand, you can sacrifice some negligible things to achieve what you want.

17

Self Esteem

$\mathcal{S}$elf esteem is essential for the positive outlooks towards facing problems. Self esteem is a path for less rutted approaches to considering events Self esteem increases self assurance in you; it helps him to give up distressing about the difficulty and help the person to overcome it with good audacity. A person becomes highly conscious of his/her requirements and makes goals and strives to meet his or her objectives.

Low Self Esteem

Cultivating pessimism or negative attitude may cause low self esteem. Low self esteem could be the result of continual tensions, workloads and enmity etc. Low self-esteem possibly will be the reason for losing self confidence. A person cannot encounter the difficulty as powerfully as he/she familiar with. Low self esteem causes despondency, lose of enthusiasm, and decline in self confidence. It can also affect the life style as well as any relations. The individual starts losing interest in actions experiencing around them, desiring to be alone and not interrelating in a team setting.

Low Self Esteem and Your Personality

Low self esteem can ruin your personality. Here are some examples of low esteem behaviour.

1. Such type of persons get wounded very easily even from a silly comment that is passed against them.
2. A person who has low self esteem feels shy to face the public.
3. Such people will be unwilling to share views and thoughts with others.
4. They prefer loneliness.
5. They get aggravated on silly matters.
6. They tend to hate who they are and find fault with themselves.
7. Such people look to pass up new experiences.
8. They may perhaps develop harmful feelings towards others.
9. They are miserable often.

10. They are scared from harmful qualms very easily.

11. The person may experience like throbbing themselves in some way.

12. Such people are very much scared that they might be deserted in a relationship.

13. Such persons may feel that they are big losers.

14. People will be afraid of confronting matters and is fearful to perform well in interviews or exams.

15. Pat yourself on your back each time you accomplish your goals. Encouraging yourself will improve your self esteem.

So, it is very much essential that one should not have low self esteem. It is equally important for a person with low self esteem to get chances to develop their self esteem and self confidence.

Ten Important Tips for Developing Your Self Esteem

Everyone wants to perk up their self esteem. Never mind if you keenly follow this aim or you subconsciously working on developing your self esteem. The difficulty with this is that in fact you unaware of what you need to develop. You are performing instinctively on external gestures.

To get an idea and to accomplish your aims faster I have framed some tips that you can use right now.

1. Improve your self esteem. You should arrange a record. What do you crave to develop or modify about the method you relate with

    development before making any more alteration.

2. Celebrate your trip, not your purpose. Try to feel good about where you are at the present, and to give off self-confidence about anyplace you may watch yourself tomorrow.

3. Set down clear objectives for yourself prior to every communication. Be aware of what you wish for. Dwell on how the public you will be meeting can facilitate you attain those objectives. Then determine how to come up to each individual accordingly. Try this frequently and you can see a difference.

4. Be pragmatic. Try to take the initiative. Be influential. Allow the other person recognise precisely how he or she can assist you.

Optimistic people will be always successful in their profession or career.

5. Give Importance. Consider per person you meet up as if she or he is really important.

6. Maintain eye contact and offer handshake; maintain a good eye contact with the person. Put into practice both of these. Your handshake must be just right. Not too hard and not too loose. Prepare yourself to become aware of something you like or feel interesting in the person.

7. Listen Properly. Train yourself to improve your listening skill. Find out a way to memorize name of other people. If you feel doubt just ask for the name again so that you can remember it always.

8. Clearly react to the other person. Smile, and address him or her by name. Enhance listening skills to clearly react. Gestures or body

practicing.

9. Listen to the other person problem with interest. Are you

filter out unpleasant news. Place yourself in the other people's shoes. Be very cautious.

10. Wait "in the moment". Never mentally detach the other person. Don't replenish at the same time as he or she speaks. What this indicates is that you must concentrate on the other person during a discussion. Anything fewer is measured impolite.

When you notice someone new, watch out for these manners. Set a mark on all these ten tips and observe how well this person has done. Possibilities are that the person got very high mark if you like her or him. In contrast the person may score very less if you don't appear to attach.

Eighteen Simple Tips for Improving Your Self Esteem

good at something. Your inventory could comprise being a close relative, a faithful buddy or a trusted worker.

questions to you. Find out as much as you can about who you are and why you feel and think the manner you perform. Self awareness is a means to success.

person who accomplishes the things you plan to carry out.

some goals at first, and achieve them.

are different from what you are and what you seem. If you allow others describe who you are, you will not get contentment. Follow your own goals - not your friend's, colleague's, or your parent's.

taking will improve your self confidence. While you take any risk: describe a clear objective. Assess the positive, realistic and possible losses.

your vocabulary each day. Undertake a new physical challenge or actions.

is very easy to develop or modify your behaviour if you think you are adorable and capable.

comments for being and performing well .

yourself dream up four optimistic ones. If you can not imagine beliefs that are correct at present next imagine beliefs you feel like to be true that you are able to do.

imagine three ways you can do to develop each of these all the more. By focusing on areas that you believe you are already perfect at will develop your self confidence and be an excellent constituent for future growth.

a confident mode.

motivating yourself and elevate your confidence level.

people.
By executing these guidelines aimed at elevating your self esteem and confidence, you can change the manner you observe yourself and the things you are able to accomplish.

18

Creativity and Innovation

*T*hink Creatively

Use a wide range of idea-creation techniques such as brainstorming etc.

Create new and worthwhile ideas both incremental and radical concepts.

Elaborate, refine, analyse and evaluate their own ideas in order to improve and maximise creative efforts.

Work Creatively with Others: Develop, implement and communicate new ideas to others effectively.

Be open and responsive to new and diverse perspectives; incorporate group input and feedback into the work.

Demonstrate originality and inventiveness in work and understand the real world limits to adopting new ideas.

View failure as an opportunity to learn; understand that creativity and innovation is a long-term, cyclical process of small successes and frequent mistakes.

Implement Innovations: Act on creative ideas to make a tangible and useful contribution to the field in which the innovation will occur.

Creative Thinking: Any primary ability or talent can be developed by training. You can improve your creative ability by exercising it.

Experience: The best creative exercises provide you with mental activity and material out of which you can form ideas. Experience can be first hand or second hand, such as reading, listening or watching. But first hand experience is far superior. A Chinese proverb states:

"I hear: I forget   I see: I remember   I do: I understand"

Travel: Traveling is a special type of first hand experience. There's no better way to broaden and refresh your outlook than travel. It gets you out of an environmental rut and exposes you to new people, customs, ideas and ways of living. One key to creative living is to view life from a fresh perspective, and travel can give you this new outlook - if you will allow it. Every culture provides a unique way of looking at common situations and solving common problems. Take photographs, keep a diary as you travel.

Self-Reliance: The more you depend on your own ability to think, the more proficient you will become at thinking up new ideas. Experts and consultants should be viewed as collaborators, not dictators. If you rely on someone else to solve your problems and tell you what to do, your creative abilities will shrivel rather than flourish for lack of exercise.

Personal Contacts: One way to learn how to think creatively is to associate yourself with creative people. Look for people who are fun to talk to and have a keen sense of interest in life. An individual who can stimulate your thought process is what you're looking for.

Children: One special group of easily accessible and highly creative people are children. It has been said that insanity is hereditary; you can get it from your children. Another thing you can get from children is a great deal of exercise. A child's world is filled with fantasy, and yours can be too, if you make the effort to interact with them.

Try the association game. You both look at something together

Playing imagination games with children and creatively interacting with them is one good way to get you back in touch with your imagination. You may even enjoy exploring the Children section of the Creativity Web.

Games and Puzzles: Certain games and puzzles can furnish you with plenty of opportunity to flex your creative muscles. The game of chess and checkers are both good games as they force you to map out strategies and make moves that depend on what your opponent does. Similar games of strategy are Shoji (Japanese Chess) and Go.

Physical sports such as football, basketball, baseball, tennis, racquetball or handball can also provide creative exercise involving strategy.

Hobbies: There are hundreds of hobbies and some of them can be real workouts for your imagination. Painting, Drawing or Sculpture can't avoid putting you creative machinery to work. Technical hobbies can also provide creative exercise, eg amateur radio, electronics, home computers.

Computers are a hobby with great potential. Think up new uses for computers in the home and write new programs to carry them out.

Reading: "Reading supplies bread for imagination to feed on, and bones for it to chew on." But not all reading is good creative exercise. The key to using reading as a creative exercise is to read selectively and actively.

Biographies can be used for creative exercise. Any life worth documenting usually involved some real imagining on the part of the subject. Perhaps you could profit from their experiences and use their creative ideas as a springboard to launch your own imagination. Another way to use reading as a creative exercise is to take a topic of interest and read several different viewpoints.

Magazines can also be used for creative exercise. Walt Disney believed in reading Reader's Digest and said:

"Your imagination may be creaky or timid or dwarfed or frozen at points. The Readers Digest can serve as a gymnasium for its training".

One of the best things about the magazine is that it provides a kaleidoscope of topics in every issue. Such diversity can provide great creative fuel.

Here is a list of just some of the contents of a Reader's Digest:

Another interest area for stimulating your imagination is to buy a different magazine each month or borrow from the library. Read something quite different to what you normally read, for example, sports, house and garden, travel, literary, gossip, fashion, comics, motoring, teenage, arts, etc.

Our brains are always working no matter what activities we are doing.Have you ever been doing one of the following activities when you suddenly had a flash of inspiration but had no means of

until a convenient time to write it down, but you found the idea had

Ideas and thoughts are fleeting and unless you catch them immediately, they will be lost. There's no way to predict when a great idea is likely to pop into your mind so you must be prepared at all times to record them. Once you have established the habit of idea recording you will be surprised at how many good ideas you actually think of each day.

Books on writing refer to your journal or your notebook. It is essential you start using a system to record your ideas, thoughts and observations. These notes will be your primary source book in your creative and humorous adventures.

So be receptive to the world around you. There are times when you may hear a snatch of conversation, or see a funny sign. Unless you capture that thought immediately, it will be gone in a matter of minutes.

It is important to be always ready for idea recording. The mind never stops chattering with all sorts of thoughts bubbling and percolating up from the subconscious mind into your conscious mind. Ideas and memories collide against each other in the subconscious melting pot and it is necessary to be ready at all times to capture those combinations that jump out. They just have to be captured. Imagine your ideas are butterflies flying out into the open. You need a net to capture the butterflies and not let them get away.

Record your Ideas: There are many other ways to record your ideas. Here are some more methods for capturing ideas:

whiteboard marker pens.

send it to your home email address.

Notepad, SimpleText or WordPad.

swimming pool.

a string. Encourage visitors to your house to add graffiti.

your home answering machine.

An Exercise in Using Idea Recording: Here is an exercise you can do to explore your challenges. Pick something from your problem bank and try one or more of these activities to capture ideas.

Speed Writing: Write a statement of your problem at the top of the page of your journal. Read it aloud three times. Then set a timer for 15 minutes and write nonstop about this problem. Think aloud by writing down your thoughts on the subject. Don't worry about spelling, grammar or sentence construction. Just keep on writing. When the time is up, review what you have written and see what ideas you can find in the writing.

Speed Talking: You will need a tape recorder or dictaphone to do this activity. Write a statement of your problem on an index card, start the recorder and read the problem aloud. Then set a timer for 15 minutes and talk non-stop about this problem. Think aloud by speaking your thoughts in a stream of words. Don't worry about making sense. Just speak your thoughts and explore any associations or side tracks.

A good way to do this exercise is to go for a walk with your dictaphone. Choose a walking route that you know will take at least 15 minutes to complete.

When you are finished, listen to the recording and write down the good ideas.

Mind Mapping: Take a piece of paper, at least A4 size, preferably bigger. Write the issue in the center of the page, summarising the issue into a key word and image. Set the timer for 15 minutes.

Draw eight lines radiating from the keyword. Start mind-mapping by writing keywords on the branches. Explore the connections and continue drawing the mind map. At the end of the time, review the mind map for ideas.

Drawing: Set a timer for ten minutes then draw a picture of your problem. Doodle and draw abstract designs. When the time is up, review the drawing to see what insights you have gained into the problem.

Vocabulary: Every time you hear a new word, write it in a special place in your journal. At the earliest opportunity, look the word up in the dictionary and write down its meaning.

Quotations: Write inspiring quotations in your journal. Choose a quotation as your theme for the day and write it in large letters.

To-do List: To-do lists are usually found in diaries, but a to-do list can be written in the journal and used as a checklist. Thomas Edison used to write to-do lists in his notebooks.

Seven Ways to Improve Your Creativity

1. Carry around a notebook with you everywhere you go. Whenever you get an idea for an article, a website, a painting - anything, write it or sketch it into the notebook. You might feel a little silly doing this, especially at first, but there is nothing quite as helpful as that notebook when you find yourself creatively strapped. All you have to do is look through the notebook for ideas that you haven't yet had time to work on. Sometimes just looking at past ideas can help you form an idea for your present problem.

2. Try coming at your problem from a new angle. If, for example, you have been commissioned to create some art for a webpage

about sports, try looking at sports from a different angle - instead of the traditional examples, think of other things that could be considered sports. Sometimes, forcing yourself to approach a problem from the exact opposite angle can be enough to spark your creativity.

3. Summarise your problem with a single and basic sentence. Let's say you have been hired to write a radio commercial for a local car dealership. Start with something basic like "car dealerships sell cars." For example, car dealerships sell cars. From there, ask yourself the 'who, what, when, where and why' of your sentence. Before you know it, you'll have pages of ideas for your commercial.

4. If all else fails, get up and walk away from your project for a while - even if you are staring in the face of an impending deadline. Go for a walk, get away from the computer - just go. Often when you feel stressed, your creativity gives way to practicality and that isn't good for someone who needs to find a fresh idea. What's more, when your brain relaxes, you'll probably find yourself flooded with ideas for your project!

5. Creativity is reduced when our seriousness is dulled. Sleep well, eat well and meditate often. I know many of us don't have the liberty of time available to mediate at home, so apply a bit of crew activity. If you have a problem with availability

minutes of meditation can put you in the right path towards becoming creative.

During this exercise, learn to breathe softly and try to relax your body completely. Once at this state, try to imagine being in a forest or any place that you like. Try visualising the surrounding in de tails. Try to listen to your surrounding and keep strolling around that place and discovering new things.

Having a hobby helps you in many ways and directly helps you in improving your creativity. It forces you to think out of the box during the period when you are conducting you're hobby. My only hobby is magic. I enjoy entertaining people and hence learn new moves and techniques all the time and spend some of my time in practicing and mastering them. You

you like and devote some time to it. You will see a remarkable improvement in your creative ability.

7. Do something which does not interest you .If you hate reading, then start reading a book. If you don't like a particular type of music, then start listening to such music. The point here is to expose your brain to as many new things and concepts as possible. You never know what new learning you might use to solve a problem later in life.

Brainstorming: The term Brainstorming has become a commonly used word in the English language as a generic term for creative thinking. The basis of brainstorming is a generating idea in a group situation based on the principle of suspending judgment - a principle which scientific research has proved to be highly productive in individual effort as well as group effort. The generation phase is separate from the judgment phase of thinking.

The term was invented by Alex Osborn and described in his book "Applied Imagination". Other authors have explained brainstorming, and I quote from Michael Morgan's book "Creative Workforce Innovation" to give the following guidelines:

Brainstorming is a process that works best with a group of people when you follow these four rules:

1. Have a well-defined and clearly stated problem
2. Have someone assigned to write down all the ideas as they occur
3. Have the right number of people in the group
4. Have someone in charge to help enforce the following guidelines:

The important thing is to have an open and receptive mind.

Twenty Characteristics of a Genius

Here is a list of twenty characteristics of Genius. Rate yourself by assigning a score of 0 to 5 for each of these qualities. Then add each of the scores to give yourself a "Genius Quotient".

1. Vision
2. Desire
3. Faith
4. Commitment
5. Planning
6. Persistence
7. Learning from mistakes

9. Mental Literacy
10. Imagination
11. Positive Attitude
12. Auto-Suggestion
13. Intuition
14. Mastermind Group (Real)
15. Mastermind Group (Internal)
16. Truth/Honesty
17. Facing Fears/Courage
18. Creativity/Flexibility
19. Love of the Task
20. Energy

Asking Questions

I keep six honest serving men,
They taught me all I knew;
Their names are What and Why and When,
And How and Where and Who.

"Just So Stories"

more times.

For example:

A fuse blew because of an overload.

There wasn't enough lubrication for the bearings.

The pump wasn't pumping enough.

The pump shaft was vibrating as a result of abrasion.

There was no filter, allowing chips of material into the pump.

Six Universal Questions

Those who generate ideas should be aware of a simple universal truth. There are only six questions that one human can ask another:

The simplest set of questions comes from the six basic questions:

19

Adaptability

 $\mathcal{A}$ daptability means to modify and adjust according to the environment and situation. For a good worker, he must have the quality to adapt and work in any environment and situation. Skills are not only pertained with the subject knowledge and talents, but also include certain soft skills like adaptability. Many soft skills are required in today's scenario to fit oneself in his workplace.

Adaptability is one of the most important soft skills that allow one to adapt or get along in most situations at work. It is the skill that is very essential to interact with supervisors, co-workers, customers and clients.

Adapting yourself with your co-workers and office environment is the first lesson that you will learn when you first join in a concern. To adapt with the colleagues you have to train yourself in the methods and ways of how to mingle with people, how to cope up with your work, how to work as a team, how to manage the stress, how to adjust with your co-workers even before you start beginning your work.

To work peacefully and comfortably in your office, a friendly environment is needed. So, how to adapt and create such a suitable environment in your office? Creating a friendly environment is not really making fun in the workplace instead it means creating or converting the workplace into a peacefully environment for work and make it better for work.

Learn the magic of how to adapt and work smoothly. Try to maintain a cordial and friendly environment in your office. Learn and teach others also the skill of adaptability.

20

Developing Good Attitude

$\mathcal{G}$ood work attitude is important for success at work. Any company or concerns that are looking for good employees and workers will look only for the person who has got good work attitude. Good work attitude is one of the important and essential aspects that a good and sincere worker must possess. One can become successful both in his work and life if he possess good attitude within himself.

Developing Good Work Attitude

Well, that is not a big trick at all, and does not have any mantras to be done or formulas to be practiced. Good work attitude can be developed and improved within you, only by self motivation and inspiration.

Here there are five such tips that may help you to improve good attitude:

1. Say You Can do it: The first quick tip in cultivating good general attitude at work is to always keep saying within your mind that I can do it. Never give a chance for any negative thoughts in your work. Never frown with the work that has been given to you. Always accept the work given to you with confidence and cheerfulness.

2. Never Say it's not Possible: Always keep in your mind that you should not say that it is not possible for you. Never underestimate yourself. Have the thought that you can achieve things in life and nothing is impossible for you.

3. Do Not Complain With Your Work: Do not complain with the work that has been given to you. Instead of wasting time sitting and complaining you can better try out the problem and finish your work. Only the coward people complain about the things they get. Always have a positive mind and work. Complaining your work may become a disease and will never allow you to progress in your work.

4. Hard Work: 'Hard Work never fails'. This is the familiar proverb that we know since our childhood. Your teacher may have told you this proverb, and to never forget this in your life time. Hard work alone will be recognised and appreciated forever. Never frame a limit in your work, instead work with all your efforts and then enjoy the fruit of hard work.

5. Plan Your Work: Planning your work will be the last tip for cultivating good work attitude. As we grow big we learn more lessons in our life. We become more experienced in life and work. So, practice the art of how to plan your work and follow that plan strictly. Initially to follow the plan may be very difficult, as you start to follow them up, you will feel easy and more comfortable with your plans.

21

Office Etiquettes

Office is the place where you spend half of the day with your co-workers. Whether younger to you or elder every colleague will be your close friends. But, you need to follow some Office Etiquette. Once in a while, it is essential to revert to basic career guidance and to send reminder of each day forgotten systems of office manners.

Always it is wrong to forget where you are, when you are at work. Certainly, there is occasion for enjoyment but by the same token, it is good to make a mistake on the part of care and be cautious with the words and deeds you apply to state yourself.

This is an art and is forgotten by everyone now days. But people forget to follow these manners, even they forget to make an eye contact or say to hello when they see their colleagues. Keep your troubles and worries aside and concentrate on the people now and again. It is not tough to accomplish and rewards far outstrip the necessary attempt.

Professional Look

Here are some tips to present yourself at job with a professional look:

DO'S:

1. Wish everyone saying good morning when you see them first time.
2. Be polite, friendly and helpful to all.
3. Dress neatly for a professional look.
4. Before enter in to your superior's or co-worker's cabin asks permission to enter in it.
5. Keep control over your emotions.
6. Respect your superiors and your co-workers.
7. Give appreciation for good works and encourage your colleagues.
8. Admit your mistakes and take responsibility for your mistakes.

9. Have a sense of humour.
10. Treat everyone equally.
11. Ask for help for any problems.
12. Accept your mistakes.
13. Take responsibility and carry out it successfully.
14. Be generous, ask if help is required
15. Admit your mistakes and ask for apology.

DON'TS:

1. Never insult your colleagues.
2. Avoid speaking harshly.
3. Don't gossip about your co-workers.
4. Don't carry your family problems to office.
5. Do not romance your co-workers.
6. Do not use alcohol or smoke at your workplace.
7. Never become a complainer.
8. Leave your work troubles at office.
9. Don't wear revealing dresses.
10. Never behave rudely to your customers.
11. Avoid selling things to your co workers.
12. Do not blame someone else if it is your fault.
13. Never be petty in your manners.
14. Do not sneeze or cough in front of your colleagues. If possible try to use tissue and say 'Excuse me'.
15. Do not give comments about a colleague's costume or look.

22

Behaving with Superiors in Your Office

$\mathcal{H}$ow you work in the office is also a part of your conduct. If every person works in harmonious way, office atmosphere is favourable to carry out better work. Bad activities form one person can ruin the office atmosphere. That is why GD (Group Discussion), communication abilities and team working are playing very important roles in achieving good jobs. Your attitude with superiors in the organisation will improve your personality and all your juniors will respect you. Superiors may have different traits but we must use smart plans in managing the officers with complicated traits.

Nine Helpful Tips

1. Never share your personal problems with your superiors and also avoid seeking advice or suggestion of your superior for solving your personal problems. Their guidance or opinions may not be likened by you and moreover you need to follow and act according to their advice, under pressure which may not be favourable to the circumstances and will get more problems to you.

2. Don't talk about your money or possessions and also about your debt to your superiors. It is always better not to be recognised by them.

3. Stay away from the gossips that are taking rounds inside your office by someone and moreover never discuss these matters with your superiors.

4. Solve all the troubles or the uncertainties about the work in office matters, which you may have with your coworkers by talking with them. If not possible, present in front of the officer and the superior in turn will resolve the matters in conference.

5. Carry out your task honestly and dedicatedly, so that you do not want to apologise to your officer often.

6. Stay away from the arguments or misinterpretations that will happen in front of the staff members.

7. Don't give assurance to anyone to execute those duties that are beyond your ability to complete. Or else you are needlessly inviting difficulties and it spoils the good name attained by you in your workplace.

8. If you face physical or emotional problems, report to your officer and talk about it with him without any hesitation. Or else, it may affect your work badly and the superior will build up bad impression regarding your working ability. So better inform this problem to your superiors.

9. If your superior is an experienced one, watch him cautiously and moreover his manner of discharging the responsibilities, it not only help you but also facilitate you in managing the office matters.

Easy Ways to Impress Your Superior

When the service recruiters select some new employees for their organisation, first they want to make sure, whether you are fit for that job or not. They would like to see your commitment to your work, they want some proof of success in similar field in the past, and they look for the person who shares the same set of value. During the first weak on the job the employer gets the full impression about you. So it's your responsibility to show your intelligence, versatility, and willingness to work and learn. The more you are enthusiastic the more you can impress them.

Here are some helpful tips:

Be Punctual: If you are on time every day, everyone will notice you and this will be an added advantage for the growth in your career. So try to be punctual.

Study Up: Try to collect the information regarding office rules, company's newsletter, annual reports and press clippings. It makes you know well about the company.

Act Happy: Everybody may have some problems at home and everyone has a bad day. Don't let the people know that you are having some problems. So try to behave as if you are pleased to be at work, even if you are not happy. Otherwise it affects your career inversely.

Look Good: Try to dress well .Think all eyes are upon you and give more attention to your dressing. If there is any dress code follow it strictly.

Show Appreciation: Be kind and appreciative to everyone who helps you.

Be Flexible: Develop flexible attitude to everything .It helps you to overcome your stress and you can easily mingle with others. It is an easy way to put good impression about you on others.

Be a Good Listener: Develop your listening skills. Pay more attention when taking some instruction from your boss and when listening the problems of colleagues

Get to Know Your Boss: Try to understand your boss's personality and work style and tailor your interactions to his or her preferences.

Be Friendly With Colleagues: Try to know more about your colleagues or those you work with you regularly. It helps you to establish a healthy relationship with them. This provides you a comfortable work atmosphere.

Identify Key Players: Identify the decision makers and influencers. Find out the traits they have in common and try to emulate them.

Take Initiative: If you completed your tasks and are ready to take heavy task, ask for more. It helps you get more impression .Always try to take initiative for your better career development.

Be a Problem Solver: Avoid rushing to your superior for silly problems. Try to solve your problems by yourself. When you face a big problem that your boss wants to know about it, then you can tell him about your problem.

Make Use of Your Time: Don't waste your time doing unnecessary things. Your time belongs to your employer, so use your time properly and concentrate on your work.

23

Coping with
Daily Distractions

There are many daily distractions like child care, elderly parents care, dull job, ill health, etc which one needs to take care of everyday. These distractions inhibit creativity. How can one cope with these distractions of daily life that deflect creativity?

Tips

Here are some tips to cope with these distractions:

- Set aside a special thinking time or thinking place. Maybe a corner of a room at home where you could indulge listening to soothing music, use or buy a flotation tank, go for jogging in the morning, take up yoga, mediation, tai-chi or some similar meditative activity.

- Get involved with children's activities; you may find that some toys aid the creative thinking process. Jig-saw puzzles (for spatial thinking), building blocks, drawing, role-playing/acting, just talking and asking questions, all contribute to creative thought and practice.

- Gaming, as a hobby, can improve problem solving and creative skills. There are many types of games that involve intellectual thought and creative solution; investigate miniatures, board games, card games, computer games and simulations, and so forth. Much creative exercise can be found in such activities.

- Try and use daily distractions to practice being creative. If you can take something dull or monotonous and play with it, it will become more interesting to you. There will be times when you can't make the extra effort, but it is very unlikely that in your entire day you can't find some activity you can make new to yourself.

- For the specific of child care - encouraging your kids' creativity along with your own would be wonderful. It will help their identity building and self-worth and will be a lot of fun if you let it. Recognise the inherent creativity in children and profit from exposure to their novel solutions to common problems in daily life.

Coping with the Challenge

The distractions of daily life can be reframed as challenges that require your creative abilities to meet. Your day-to-day routines afford the most common opportunities for you to be creative. In fact, if you take stock of a typical week, you will find that you have indeed been very creative in solving many of the problems that confront you. Of course, we tend not to notice this. You may even tell yourself that what you do is not creative at all. Be careful what you tell yourself. You may begin believing it.

Coping with the distractions and necessities of daily life is a major challenge for most of us. But just as we find the time to eat and sleep, we need to find the time to ignite our creativity. Is it not possible to find one hour per day to spend exploring our talents and

Losing our creative energies due to the distractions of daily life has a lot to do with focal and conscious attention. In our very stressful society, we do not learn much about focusing attentively and retrospectively onto something, onto what we are doing. Meditation can be a very good way to help to be more attentive and thus creative.

I heard a story about a doctor's office that placed large nuts and bolts in their waiting room and found that none complained about waiting.

If you want to relax....go fishing.

Learn to incorporate the imagination into every activity, to use your creative talents to improve your daily life.

24

Your Career Success Equation

$\mathcal{C}$areer success is a function of three factors, which are all equally important. These factors are:

% Success = Ability X Environment X Effort: Always it is wrong to forget where you are, when you are at work. Certainly, there is occasion for enjoyment but by the same token, it is good to make a mistake on the part of care and be cautious with the words and deeds you apply to state yourself.

This is an art and is forgotten by everyone now days. But people forget to follow these manners, even they forget to make an eye contact or say to hello when they see their colleagues. Keep your troubles and worries aside and concentrate on the people now and again. It is not tough to accomplish and rewards far outstrip the necessary attempt. If you remember your maths, you will know that any number times zero equals zero, thus all of those three factors should be on your side.

1. Ability = Talent + Skills: Ability consists of two aspects, your talent which comes naturally to you, and your skills, which is what you have learned through training and development, whether in formal programs of study or on-the-job experiential learning. If you have talent in an area, it makes sense to focus your learning on ways to further develop skills that enable you to profit from your natural talents.

Certain aspects of your personality, which are a function of your particular psychological needs, tend to remain fairly constant over time. The Personal Orientation Profile™ test, which I use to assess career aptitudes, measures these personality traits. Most of the scores stay the same thus those aspects of you can be considered talents. Indeed, if you use the information from the test to make intelligent career choices, you will find that any character trait can be strength in one situation or environment, and a weakness in another. The test is not about good or bad scores; no one passes or fails. It is about finding a good match between an organisation's culture, with the specific job requirements, and your needs.

2. Environment = S + W + O + T: Environment as it relates to your career prospects can be assessed using, what is called in organisation behaviour and business management programs, a SWOT analysis. SWOT stands for strengths, weaknesses, opportunities, and threats. Think of the first two as being your internal environment. When you consider a particular career path, what are your strengths and weaknesses relative to the demands of that job, that industry segment, the corporate culture of companies

where you can capitalise on your strengths, and where you can minimise the negative impact of your weaknesses, and hopefully continue to grow and develop your abilities.

The latter two relate to the external environment. Economic, political, social/cultural, industry competition, government regulatory issues, your contacts and connections: you have many factors to consider when you look at what threats and opportunities are in store for you! The very circumstances which create economic threats for people in one field would present opportunities for people in a different field. Thus it is really worthwhile to keep abreast of what is going on, in your local community as well as a wider scope.

Get your information from as many different places as possible, so that you get a balanced view; you don't want to be overly influenced in any one direction by having only a single source! Try to gain a perspective on what the needs are out there, so you can imagine ways of filling those needs. Whether it's reading trade magazines that relate to your interests, or articles in the life section that tell you about trends, there is information easily and freely available to you.

So once you have assessed your abilities, your strengths and weaknesses, and come to terms with both those aspects of yourself which you probably cannot change, and the external environment with its threats and opportunities, you need to make a fundamental

3. Effort

The only part of the success equation that is 100% under your control is the Effort. Think about your life for a moment. You will notice that you can easily give 100% effort with certain activities, which hold a great deal of interest for you, or for which you have natural aptitude. Other tasks you find too boring or too difficult or not challenging or interesting enough, so you neglect them or only give part of your energy to it. Clearly, it will be easier to motivate yourself to give your best if you can get more clarity about where your values are, what your long term goals are, and how your working life aligns with your personal life.

Another factor which influences your ability to make a sustained effort is your overall energy level. You can improve this by learning effective stress management techniques, and by improving your nutrition habits.

Be the Best in Your Job

Many people feel their job is unrewarding and unrelated to their goals. I believe that you will be a happier and a more successful person if you adopt the principle of always giving your best, even in the more menial of jobs you might be hired for.

Moreover, if you are busy being the best cook or sales officer or secretary or whatever, you are bound to connect with someone who will recognise you as a person with potential, i.e. as someone who is committed to giving value rather than just collecting a paycheck. If you have clear goals and you give your best, you will inevitably attract the attention of people who have power, position and influence. Hence they will want to makes better use of your talents.

Finally this book can help you assess yourself, upgrade desired skills and teach you how to adapt to work environment. But it is only you who will decide on your priorities and objectives; create a personal action plan to head in the right direction; to get information and make connections to create a network of people that could help you achieve your goals.

Remember it is only YOU who can decide how much effort you would like to make to create the life you want.

Annexure

Must Read Popular Books

*W*ho Moved My Cheese? An Amazing Way to Deal with Change in Your Work and in Your Life by Spencer Johnson (Putnam Publishing Group, 1998)

Change can be a blessing or a curse, depending on your perspective. The message of this book is that all can come to see it as a blessing, if they understand the nature of cheese and the role it plays in their lives. Who Moved My Cheese is a parable that takes place in a maze. The point of the story is that we have to be alert to changes in the cheese, and be prepared to go running off in search of new sources of cheese when the cheese we have runs out.

Paradoxical Thinking by Jerry Fletcher & Kelle Olwyler (Berrett-Koehler Publishers, 1997)

The book takes the mystery and unpredictability out of performing at your peak by providing an easy-to-learn method of understanding and maximising your personal success. It gives practical advice for sorting out tough choices and taking action to resolve them.

A Peacock in the Land of Penguins by Barbara Hateley (Berrett-Koehler, San Francisco, 1995)

A short and rather light fable, this book celebrates the value of diversity. Openness to diverse styles and cultures is one important side of Adaptability competency.

The Situational Leader by Paul Hersey (Prentice-Hall, 1985)

This is the classic book on the theory of situational leadership. It proposes that there is no one best leadership style for all occasions and hence a key to leadership is adaptability.

A Force For Change: How Leadership Differs From Management by John P. Kotter

This classic book is about how leadership is different from management.

Breakthrough Thinking : The Seven Principles of Creative Problem Solving 2nd edition by Gerald Nadler (Prima Publishing, 1996) :

This book presents some novel ideas on how to approach problems based on the thought processes of great thinkers. It includes exercises you can do to practice their suggested approach.